ippr

DEPARTMENT OF
POLITICS
AND
INTERNATIONAL
RELATIONS

TIME FOR LAND VALUE TAX?

EDITED BY DOMINIC MAXWELL AND ANTHONY VIGOR

ippr

The **Institute for Public Policy Research** (ippr) is the UK's leading progressive think tank and was established in 1988. Its role is to bridge the political divide between the social democratic and liberal traditions, the intellectual divide between academia and the policy making establishment and the cultural divide between government and civil society. It is first and foremost a research institute, aiming to provide innovative and credible policy solutions. Its work, the questions its research poses and the methods it uses are driven by the belief that the journey to a good society is one that places social justice, democratic participation and economic and environmental sustainability at its core.

For further information you can contact ippr's external affairs department on info@ippr.org, you can view our website at www.ippr.org and you can buy our books from Central Books on 0845 458 9910 or email ippr@centralbooks.com.

Our trustees

CONTENTS

Acknowledgements

The editors would like to thank the pamphlet's contributors for their good nature in responding to our editorial advice and deadlines. We would also like to thank Will Paxton and Stuart White for their roles in helping to start the project, all of those who attended the seminar held at Oxford University. Thanks to the Departmant of Politics and International Relations at Oxford University in particulsr the Public Policy Unit and ARCO for financial assistance in making this publication possible. Within ippr we would like to thank the following: John Adams, Jim Bennett, Tony Grayling, Adam Marshall, Nick Pearce, Sonia Sodha, Kate Stanley, Howard Reed, Peter Robinson.

This document emerged from a series of seminars on the New Politics of Ownership commissioned by Stuart White, University of Oxford and Will Paxton, then at the ippr. The final papers from those seminars will be published in January 2006 by The Policy Press under the title *The Citizen's Stake: The future of universal asset policies*.

About the authors

Richard Brooks is Research Director for the Fabian Society.

Dominic Maxwell is a Research Fellow in the social policy team at ippr.

Iain McLean is Professor of Politics at the University of Oxford, Official Fellow in Politics, Nuffield College, and Director of the Public Policy Unit, Department of Politics & International Relations, Oxford University.

John Muellbauer is Professor of Economics, University of Oxford and Official Fellow in Economics, Nuffield College.

Anthony Vigor is a Research Fellow in the sustainability team at ippr.

Karl Widerquist is a Doctoral Candidate in Politics at Lady Margaret Hall.

1. Introduction

Dominic Maxwell and Anthony Vigor, Institute for Public Policy Research

If it ain't broke, don't fix it – but the problem is being sure when it's broken. The current structure of property taxes in the UK, outlined in Table 1, below, does not adequately promote government objectives. Could this be addressed by the introduction of a Land Value Tax (LVT)? And if so, how do we manage the process of transition? This pamphlet sets out to answer these two questions. Debate around the merits and failings of LVT has been conducted largely outside the mainstream of political debate. We want to open up the debate, expose it to a wider audience and to more difficult questions around implementation and practicability. It includes contributions from two internationally-renowned academics, Professors John Muellbauer and Iain McLean. Richard Brooks, Research Director of the Fabian Society, provides a political perspective on the implementation of LVT, and Karl Widerquist summarises the discussion at a seminar held in Oxford on the subject.

This introduction outlines the problems with the current property taxation system, and why these problems have become particularly relevant now. It moves on to suggest how LVT may be able to provide part of a solution, and ends with summaries of the other chapters.

As well as the dedicated property taxes below, property is affected by income tax and corporation tax on rental yields, and by "Section 106 Agreements". Named after the legislation that enables them, these are paid by developers to local authorities to mitigate the impact of development – for example, they may contribute towards the costs of new roads, or, more commonly, social housing.

Table 1: The current property taxation system and annual revenues (2004-05 estimates)

Council Tax
An annual tax on domestic property set by local authorities. It replaced the Community Charge (Poll Tax) in 1991. The tax rate varies according to the property's value within eight bands and the rate of tax set by Local Authorities. These bands are based on 1991 valuations.
£19.8bn

National Non-Domestic Rates
Levied on businesses and other occupiers of non-domestic property. Increases in the yield from business rates are fixed at the rate of price inflation, and the rate was nationalised in 1990 (a different rate applies in Scotland). The tax is levied against assessed rental values, which are revalued every five years.
£19.0bn

Stamp Duty
Land Tax Levied on the purchase and lease of domestic property. It is charged as a proportion of the property's cost. Properties between £120,000 and £250,000 pay 1%; £250,001-£500,000 pay 3%; and over £500,001, 4%.
£6.3bn

Inheritance Tax
A tax paid at death on an 'estate' (essentially everything an individual owns, as well as some assets given away before death). The tax is not levied on estates worth less than £275,000. The rate is 40%.
£2.9bn (although it is worth noting that not all of this revenue is from property)

Capital Gains Tax
A tax on any increase in value of an asset, levied at point of sale. This does not apply to personal belongings worth £6,000 or less or, in most cases, a principal private residence.
£2.3bn (again it is worth noting that not all of this revenue is from property)

Sources: Direct.gov (2005); HMRC (2005); HM Treasury (2005); VOA (2005)

Inaction is not an option

All systems of taxation have secondary effects, such as giving incentives to consume some goods rather than others. At a time when one of the government's priorities is to increase the level of housebuilding (ODPM, 2005; HMT and ODPM, 2005) it is sensible to review the taxes that affect property and land to see whether they are contributing to this goal. The papers presented in this pamphlet suggest they are undermining it. This section argues that the current taxes are failing in three areas:

- Frustrating development and infrastructure funding,
- Weakening rather than promote macroeconomic stability,
- Imposing arbitrary burdens on certain tax-payers.

Taxes must also meet more general principles of good taxation, outlined in Table 2.

Table 2: Principles of good taxation

- Horizontal equity: If people are the same, treat them the same way.
- Vertical equity: If people are different, treat them differently. Which differences and similarities count as relevant is never clear-cut, but the general rule is to recognise and make allowances for involuntary differences in situation, but not differences that result from choice.
- Minimal deadweight loss: When a tax is levied on a good, the price received by the seller is lower than that paid by the buyer. This prevents some sales from taking place, even if they

would otherwise increase welfare. The net loss of utility is known as a "deadweight loss", or excess burden.

- Minimal distortion of incentives: The tax wedge that creates a deadweight loss also distorts incentives. The degree of distortion depends on the marginal tax rate, rather than average rate.
- Minimal collection and administration costs The tax process should be as simple as possible for tax collection authorities.
- Minimal compliance costs The tax process should be as simple as possible for the taxpayer.

Adapted from: Atkinson and Stiglitz (1980) and Kay and King (1990)

The current system: frustrating development and infrastructure funding

Local communities sometimes feel they are penalised for economic success and population growth. An expanding population places extra burdens on local services and infrastructure, while the current system for gathering and allocating resources fails to keep pace. This has led some (Cheshire and Sheppard, 2004) to suggest that planning mechanisms distort the incentives of decision-makers, presenting them with the costs of development but directing the benefits elsewhere as central government claims much of any increased tax revenue. Travers (2005) argues that this centralised fiscal system frustrates local growth and innovation. The recent Local Authority Business Growth Initiative innovation – designed to encourage local authorities to promote economic development by retaining some of the associated increase in business rates – only operates at the margins of any real reform, and does little to change the centralised taxation system (see Marshall, cited in Gardiner, 2005).

Yet public investment in infrastructure does generate significant gains. The problem is that these flow to private property owners, rather than being captured by property taxes and returned to the public purse. London's Jubilee Line Extension is often cited as a prime example. Costing £3.5 billion of public money to build, a TfL-commissioned report suggested that around Canary Wharf and Southwark tube stations alone, the up-lift in land value attributable to the extension was £2.8 billion (Atisreal and Geofutures, 2005). Other studies have put the overall up-lift figure along the whole extension nearer £10 billion (Riley, 2001). If we were better able to capture these increases in land value – increases that occur through no effort or risk on behalf of the private individual – it is likely that the funding delays over new major infrastructure projects such as Crossrail and localised delays in new development could be avoided (Huhne, 2004).

The current level of infrastructure investment threatens the government's housebuilding objectives (South East Commission, 2005). One report claimed there is an £8 billion pound gap in public resources to provide the necessary infrastructure in the South East alone (Roger Tyms and Partners, 2005). While this figure should be treated with caution as it is very difficult to put exact figures on projected infrastructure costs, it is clear that the government's ambitions on housing growth – and the provision of affordable housing and transport infrastructure especially – are running up against funding issues. As Figure 1 shows, public spending on transport and housing as a proportion of GDP is only recently returning to the levels of the mid-1990s, and lower than in the early 1990s. There is a live question about whether it will be possible to deliver an ambitious housing policy agenda with public resources at two-thirds of the level of national income devoted in the early 1990s (Vigor and Robinson, 2005).

Figure 1: Public spending on transport and housing as a percentage of gross domestic product, 1989-2008

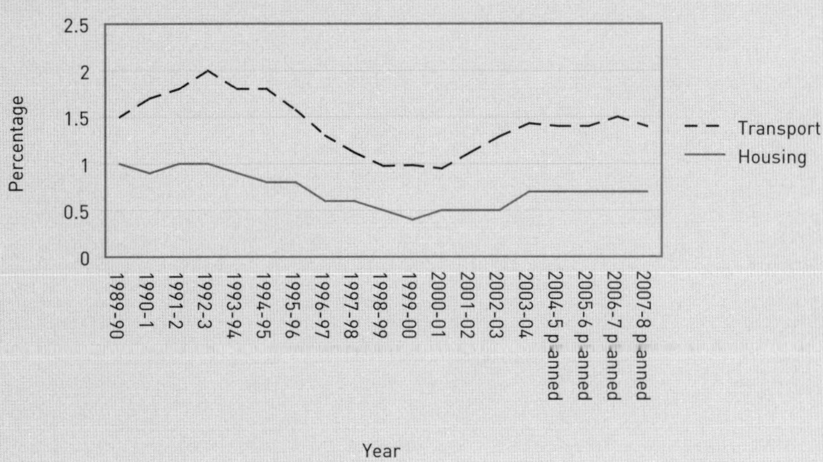

Source: HMT and ONS (2004) and HMT (2004)

New developments currently contribute to infrastructure provision through Section 106 agreements, as mentioned above. These agreements are negotiated between local authorities and developers and help mitigate the impact of new development and finance local infrastructure. The two most comprehensive surveys of Section 106 show that while it is an increasingly important mechanism for delivering affordable housing, it will not make up the shortfall in public spending (Monk *et al.*, 2005; Crook *et al.*, 2002). Monk *et al.* (2005) indicated that 91 per cent of dwellings provided through Section 106 also receive public grant – and this figure is higher in the higher-cost growth areas. It is unsurprising in this context that there is a growing interest in other potential sources of infrastructure funding.

Interest focuses on two areas. First, the government is looking into the Planning-gain Supplement PGS recommended by the Barker Review (Barker, 2004), with both the Deputy Prime Minister, John Prescott, MP and the Minister for Housing and Planning, Yvette Cooper, MP recently signalling their support (Porter, 2005; Weaver 2005). Second, others are looking to introduce a development 'tariff', or 'roof tax', where developers are charged a fixed price per new dwelling, with the aim of providing the funding for necessary infrastructure locally in an efficient manner (Planning Resource, 2005). Although these are potentially useful innovations, they may serve to disincentivise development: they tax new buildings directly. A Planning-gain Supplement will capture value up-lift in new developments only, rather than in all property that benefits from the investment. There may be a better solution.

Undermining economic stability

As well as these funding and spending considerations, there is a concern that the current taxation system threatens macroeconomic stability. As Barker (2003) points out, the year-to-year volatility of the UK housing market is unexceptional: close to Italy and Belgium, higher than Germany and France, but lower than Spain, the Netherlands and Sweden. But the UK is unusual in the degree to which house prices affect the rest of the economy – the correlation between house-price inflation and consumption in the UK is more than twice that of Germany, and a third higher than in France. As Muellbauer points out in this volume, "concern with macroeconomic stability is not an arcane academic curiosum", but is crucial to firms and individuals.

Unstable prices can be calmed by more responsive demand. If higher property prices lead to higher taxes, then the incentives to use existing land and property more efficiently are sharpened. There is a higher cost of holding developable land or under-used, particularly in more expensive areas, and so supply becomes more responsive. But the current property taxes do not do this – or at least, not well. They fail to track adequately difference over time, between regions, or between properties, thereby letting the structural instability continue unchecked. This is partly a problem with infrequent revaluations. But it is also embedded in the regressive banding of Council Tax, which weakens the relationship between property value and tax liability.

By imposing taxes on purchases, rather than value, stamp duty also reduces the incentive to move out of large, expensive housing in order to release equity, again reducing the responsiveness of supply. Barker (2003) may be right that stamp duty is overshadowed by equity gains in a buoyant market, but it contributes to an already considerable moving cost – especially for homes large enough to release equity, and those in expensive areas such as London and the South East. After paying for the land registry, solicitor fees, removal fees, and survey costs, an additional charge between one and four percent of the value of the house is far from insignificant.[1]

Imposing arbitrary losses

The efficiency losses of the current stamp duty system are compound by equity problems. Crossing a tax threshold increases the rate for the entire price, rather than just the top slice, so haggling the sale price of your home up by £1, from £119,999 to £120,000, incurs a £1,200 tax penalty. A similar jump occurs at each boundary: the last pound of sales at £250,000 and £500,000 both push the tax bill up by £5,000. These spikes create perverse incentives, arbitrary losers and a culture of avoidance. They are simply poor design.

But the problems of stamp duty, severe as they are, are overshadowed by the flaws in its companion property tax, council tax. Its failure to reflect differences between properties means it hits the poorest hardest: the poorest fifth of households pay five per cent of their household income in council tax; the middle fifth pay three per cent; and the richest fifth pay under two percent (National Statistics, 2005). And as Muellbauer points out in his contribution, the fact that the tax changes so little between areas means that it represents a far lower proportion of land value in richer areas.

The property tax system in the UK causes problems for development, stability, and equity. But these problems are not new: why should we tackle them now?

A window of opportunity

Significant elements of property taxation are currently under review. Does this provide a chance to consider significant reform?

The government is currently considering its response to the Barker Review, with the introduction of the Planning-gain Supplement looking likely. Additionally, the Lyons Inquiry has been established in response to the government's recent Balance of Funding Review (ODPM, 2004), "to consider the case for changes to the present system of local government funding in England and to make recommendations, including on the reform of council tax" (Lyons Inquiry, 2004). The Lyons Inquiry is therefore looking at two key issues – the revaluation of council tax and the balance of funding between local and central government. Initially due to report in

---

1 Further research is required on the issue of whether the buyer or the seller actually pays SDLT. The extent to which the tax can be passed on (through lower offers) depends on how demand and supply respond to price changes.

2005, the government has postponed the Inquiry's final report until after the next General Election.

This inquiry is driven in part by political considerations. Council tax revaluation in 2007 will lead to winners and losers, with many of the latter group concentrated in key South East constituencies. Similarly, the appropriate balance of funding between local and central government is a perennial debate and is tied up with questions of local autonomy and central control. These are significant structural governmental issues and early press reports suggest that Lyons is attempting to play down hopes of radical reform (Blitz, 2005).

So, together there seems only a limited appetite for reform. Is this a missed opportunity? The next section will identify what Land Value Taxation is and how it may be an appropriate way of addressing some of the concerns highlighted above.

Land Value Tax: a better way?

Land Value Taxation is an annual tax on the market rental value of land. It would be levied as a fixed rate. It taxes the given value of the land, not the development that has occurred on it, and does so whether or not the land has been sold. It has, therefore, a number of advantages over other forms of taxation and addresses a number of the concerns raised above, especially incentives, equity and economic efficiency.

As an annual charge on the rental value of the land, LVT would not be a tax on transactions and therefore development. As outlined above, not only would this conflict less with government policy to deliver an increase in the rate of housebuilding, it could actively promote it by providing incentives for local authorities to encourage development. An annual tax on the market rental value of the land – levied regardless of the land use or development on it – would further promote the re-use of brownfield land because a vacant site would still incur an annual charge. Indeed, some argue it could also promote more sustainable patterns of development by encouraging businesses to locate in less prosperous regions as the market value of land would be lower compared to more prosperous regions (LVT Campaign, 2002; and Muellbauer, chapter three below).

LVT also has the benefit of capturing the increases in private wealth that accrue through public investment. As an annual fixed rate, revenues would rise as the land's market value (and therefore tax base) increases. In theory, therefore, there it could provide an automatic revenue stream to help fund infrastructure projects.

There is the need for some caution, however. Forms of land taxation have been tried before, in the form of development taxes. As Table 3 outlines, there have been four attempts since World War Two. These previous taxes have aimed to capture windfall gains from both the granting of planning permission and also in the case of the Development Land Tax, from development itself. Many reasons have been advanced for their failure. Some complain of their complexity and the fact that none of them were given time to bed-in (Connellan and Lichfield, 2000). Others also point to the fact that developers and landowners often waited for legal challenges to be cleared up or a change of government (usually from Labour to Conservative) as there was widespread opposition amongst this group and within Parliament (Barker, 2003). Again, the LVT advocates' argument here is that taxing development is inappropriate.

Table 3: Past UK examples of land taxation

Tax	Levy	Years of operation
Development Land Tax	100% of the value uplift in land value due to the granting of planning permission.	1947-1953
Betterment Levy	40%, due to rise through time to encourage early sale, again designed to capture value uplift. Capital Gains Tax was also introduced in 1967 to capture increases in the existing use value of land only.	1967-1971
Development Gains Tax	An interim tax on the capital gains derived from the disposal of land and buildings with development value or potential.	1974
Development Land Tax	Taxed development gain – i.e. the difference between the net proceeds after disposal of development and either the current use value of land or the cost of land acquisition (whichever was higher)	1976-1985

Source: adapted from Connellan and Lichfield (2000)

Indeed, advocates often point to Denmark and New Zealand as examples where LVT has worked, with both introducing quite radical schemes in the nineteenth Century. However, both countries have recently removed their major forms of LVT and retain less radical property taxation (Andelson, 2000). Keall (2000) suggests that New Zealand's national land tax was removed in

1991 due to a combination of practical issues and political expediency. It is useful to reflect on this experience. Practically, 1989 saw a significant, but short-lived, increase in commercial land values (especially in Auckland and Wellington). The routine land value assessment that informed the tax rate setting occurred during this peak. The tax levied the next year – during a more modest land value period – was therefore based on these inflated prices and provoked a backlash which the incumbent Labour Government reacted to by removing the tax (and increased taxes on goods and services).

Despite these and the UK's setbacks LVT should not necessarily be dismissed. A number of other countries use forms of LVT as part of their fiscal framework – South Africa, some Caribbean states and Western Canada, for example. Slightly different systems operate in Hong Kong and Singapore where all and most land, respectively, is publicly owned and therefore rent flows directly to the state.

Radical reform, not sudden reform

All of these arguments point to the need for reform of how property is taxed in Britain. Simply revaluing homes and introducing a Planning-gain Supplement will not prevent these problems from recurring. But radical reform does not mean sudden reform, and the political and logistical barriers to LVT make it a distant goal at best. To make LVT achievable, we must plan how to get there.

Firstly, the current tinkering should be publicly acknowledged as a stepping stone, not a destination. Simply by announcing in which direction it wishes to travel, the government has the power to focus debate and engage the thoughts and experiences of academics and professionals. It is clear from the previous attempts at land taxation that building a cross-party political consensus is also important. ippr's recent cross-party Commission on Sustainable Development did exactly this, arguing: "a land value tax could well be a useful tool for delivering sustainable development, as long as any future reform recognises two fundamental factors. First, new development must be incentivised. Second, extra resources are required to meet housing needs within the South East" (South East Commission, 2005: 55).

Secondly, the details of upcoming reform should be designed with a more ambitious goal in mind. Returning to the problems described at the start of this introduction tells us what changes are needed.

To create an automatic stabiliser for the housing market, existing property taxes must respond better to differences over time, between regions, and between properties. Making revaluation an annual process and creating more bands would go some way towards achieving this.

More volatile property taxes require us to pay more attention to the asset-rich income-poor. Letting pensioners defer tax until they move house or die is one option, although more analysis is needed of who would benefit, and how much it would have to be funded by government. It would also require sensitive handling, as shown by coverage of the same proposal for Northern Ireland, in August 2005. After quoting John Muellbauer on the benefits of deferral, the *Daily Mail* dubbed deferred taxation a "death tax" that would "dash many children's hopes of inheriting the home they grew up in" (Doughty 2005).

To capture some of the private profit from public infrastructure investment, the relationship between central and local government will have to be addressed. The postponement of the Lyons Inquiry's final report provides the opportunity to start from a question of what local government is for, and then how should it be financed, rather than the political fire-fighting that Lyons was previously engaged with. At a time when local authorities are being encouraged to bring forward housing growth and play a bigger role in economic development, it would seem sensible that they have fiscal mechanisms to enable this.[2] Reassessing the role of equalisation grants and identifying ways local authorities can better capture the gains from development would seem sensible here.

The Planning-gain Supplement, proposed by Barker (2004) and likely to be adopted by the government, establishes the principle that some increases in value arise from public action, rather than private, and that it is therefore legitimate for it to be used for the public good. This principle must be articulated. PGS should be used as a "wedge issue", expanding the space in which the idea is accepted (see, for example, Lakoff 2005), and making it easier to apply it more widely. The government must therefore base its arguments for a PGS firmly and publicly on principles, rather than the pragmatic need for funds.

Finally, in the longer term, a change in the tax system presents an opportunity to iron out the arbitrary jumps in stamp duty. Simply changing from a "slab" structure to a tapered one, so that higher rates would apply only to the additional pound over a threshold, would impose a considerable cost to the exchequer. Every house over £120,000 would pay £1,200 less tax, every house over £250,000 would pay £6,200 less, and over £500,000, £11,200 less. Attempting to recover this revenue through a new top-rate would prove politically difficult, particularly as Labour has already increased the top rate by three percentage points. A new system entirely, such as LVT, would provide an opportunity to iron out the jumps whilst retaining fiscal neutrality.

There does not seem to be the political appetite for significant reform of property taxation. Yet it is clear that property taxation does not currently efficiently or equitably promote government objectives. 2005 is an important year in the property taxation debate. The government's response to the Barker Review and the on-going Lyons Inquiry should not serve to close off

2 ippr's Centre for Cities is currently running a City Leadership project looking at this question. Further information can be obtained from: www.ippr.org/centreforcities

debate on more profound reform of property taxation. This is not a call for a revolution in taxation. We are not what Andelson (2000: xix) has termed 'whole-hoggers', we do not believe that LVT is "the sovereign path to social justice." The wholesale replacement of swathes of the existing taxation system with LVT (as recommended recently by Harrison, 2004) is likely to cause significant costs in terms of economic instability. Rather, there is a role for a LVT within a broader fiscal framework. Barker's (2004) tentative suggestion for an LVT on brownfield land provides a closer model. The chapters that follow offer some positive suggestions.

Structure of this pamphlet

Iain McLean: The politics of land tax – then and now

Iain McLean, in chapter two, outlines the classical arguments for LVT: Tom Paine, who argued that land was originally unowned and is therefore taxable; and David Ricardo, who introduced the concept of economic "rent" deriving its value from scarcity rather than investment. The arguments for a land tax were widely spread by Henry George (1879), culminating in never-implemented proposals in Lloyd George's budgets of 1909 and 1914.

McLean then turns to the practicalities of LVT today, answering a number of possible objections. The failure of previous attempts does not show that land tax is unfeasible in principle, only that it should be based on capital value rather than transactions. Previous attempts gave property owners the chance to delay transactions in the hope that their lobbying against the legislation would succeed. Assessment and revaluation is currently problematic only because too long elapses between valuations, creating large incentives to block the process amongst those whose assets have risen in relative value. That a land tax would penalise the "asset-rich cash-poor", such as pensioners, can be solved by allowing them to defer the tax liability until death – and by pointing out that people should face the real opportunity cost of continuing to live in large houses. And finally, the notion that such a tax would give councillors an incentive to permit sprawling developments can be answered by saying that the ballot box is exactly the place where such trade-offs should be decided.

The chapter then moves to the political prospects for reform. LVT could replace the current raft of bad property taxes: stamp duty, inheritance tax, and – more tentatively – council tax. McLean also recommends replacing National Non-Domestic Rates (NNDR also known as Uniform Business Rates) with LVT. A single rate for business and residential houses would shift the burden from companies to individuals, so it is necessary to add the constraint that in its first year LVT on business should yield the same as NNDR, and LVT on houses the same as council tax. Operational land – roads, railway track, sewage farms – could be exempted, farms would be below the starting threshold, and a "public-benefit" exemption could be applied to other lands if the public had sufficient access to them.

McLean sees LVT as a tool for local rather than central government. It would encourage them to make the best use of land on their patch, and unlike other tax bases it does not move and cannot be hidden.

McLean recommends that in the interim, policymakers could prepare the way by making council tax less regressive, announce an intention to introduce a fairer system for 2009, and scrap Section 106 Agreements and the Local Authority Business Growth Incentive.

John Muellbauer: Property taxation and the economy

John Muellbauer, in chapter three, makes a strong economic case for LVT on businesses, and market-based property taxes for households. He points to the central role of the "bubble builder", or "momentum", in driving property prices, which means that high returns tend to be followed by further high returns, and national and local overshooting of property prices is endemic. This causes two problems.

The first problem is macroeconomic instability. Linking property and land taxes to current or recent house prices, throughout the property price cycle, would go some way to resolving the problem. It would tend to soften recessions, and prevent bubbles by choking off further demand when house prices rise relative to imputed rents and incomes. On the supply side, market-based property taxes and LVT would sharpen the incentives not to keep property vacant or under-occupied. Existing buildings make up approximately 99 per cent of effective supply, so making the existing stock even slightly more responsive to prices has a greater effect than improving the responsiveness of new build.

The second problem caused by the "momentum" of house prices is that it leads to resource misallocation: investing in housing is less profitable in areas where house prices are falling, leading to vicious downward price spirals. This failure of prices to signal scarcity also exacerbates the problems of congested successful locations. The regional and local regressiveness of council tax contributes to the problem by imposing on the poorest areas the highest tax per pound of land value.

Muellbauer suggests replacing council tax with a property tax. For households, a sensible rate for the UK is probably of the order of half a per cent of value, with pensioners able to postpone payment until death or the sale of property. The tax should be primarily national, not local, as central government is better able to cope with a relatively unstable source of revenue. Central government could in return transfer a share of its income tax to local government.

For businesses, half of the basis for NNDR, could be shifted from business assets to land value. A certain value per hectare, say, £20,000, could be exempt, thereby excluding most farmland. To ease cashflow a payment window of three to five years could be allowed, and the reforms would have to be phased in gradually. In return, stamp duty could switch to a simple two per cent flat rate, or properly tapered with a two per cent maximum.

Muellbauer finishes by contrasting his proposals with those contained in the Barker Review.

Muellbauer and McLean do not entirely agree. McLean suggests that the current property tax for businesses, NNDR, should be entirely converted to a land tax. Muellbauer would shift only half the basis to land tax, keeping the other half on property. For houses, McLean concludes that, although the case for LVT is strong, the political problems of transition may make it "a step too far". Muellbauer shares no such compunction: he proposes a tax on property (not land) of around half of one per cent.

The most significant disagreement is over whether the taxes should be local or national. For McLean, it should be local: real estate is fixed in a given location, and a local LVT would encourage local authorities to make the best use of it. Muellbauer suggests that a domestic property tax would be a relatively unstable source of revenue, and the central government is better able to cope with fluctuations. He proposes that 75 per cent of the revenue should go to central government, and that, in return, central government should relocate some income tax to local government.

Richard Brooks: The politics of transition

Richard Brooks, in chapter four, examines the political problems associated with the move to LVT, and suggests some ways round them. The arguments for LVT can be integrated with existing discussions around council tax revaluation, an over-heated housing market, and the Lyons Inquiry. All of these require a political sensitivity to both those most likely to be affected by any change and the public acceptance of taxes on assets (also see Maxwell, 2004). This provides some important challenges for preparing the ground, including softening some of the impacts of a land tax, even if this means losing some of the economic benefits. Perhaps the most important research would be a clear understanding of the household impacts. Ultimately, no scheme which appears to be financially detrimental to significant numbers of swing voters in marginal constituencies is politically plausible.

Karl Widerquist: Summary of debate.

Karl Widerquist provides the summary of a seminar held jointly by ippr and Oxford University at which the previous three papers were presented. Concerns and suggestions focused on the distributional impact, the local/national balance of LVT, and the lessons we should take from international experiences.

References

Andelson, R V (2000). "Introduction", in Andelson RV (ed) *Land-Value Taxation Around the World*. Third Edition. Oxford: Blackwell.

Atisreal and Geofutures (2005). *Property Value Study – assessing the change in values attributable to the Jubilee Line Extension*. London: Transport for London.

Atkinson, AB and Stiglitz, JE (1980) *Lectures on Public Economics*, Maidenhead: McGraw-Hill

Barker, K (2004). *Barker Review of Housing Supply: securing our future housing needs*. Final Report. London: HM Treasury and Office of the Deputy Prime Minister.

Barker, K (2003). *Barker Review of Housing Supply: securing our future housing needs*. Interim Report. London: HM Treasury and Office of the Deputy Prime Minister.

Blitz, R (2005). "Adviser plays down council tax reform". *Financial Times*, 6th July. Accessed online: www.ft.com.

Brown, Gordon (1997). "Exploiting the British genius – the key to long-term economic success". Speech to the Confederation of British Industry, 20 May. www.hm-treasury.gov.uk/newsroom_and_speeches/speeches/-chancellorexchequer/ speech_chex_200597.cfm.

Cheshire, P and Sheppard, S (2005). "The introduction of price signals into land use planning decision-making: a proposal." *Urban Studies* 42(4), 647-663.

Connellan, C and Lichfield, N (2000). "Great Britain", in Andelson RV (ed) *Land-Value Taxation Around the World*. Third Edition. Oxford: Blackwell.

Crook, T; Currie, J; Jackson, A; Monk, S; Rowley, S; Smith, K and Whitehead, C (2002). *Planning Gain and Affordable Housing: making it count*. York: Joseph Rowntree Foundation.

Directgov (2005) *Money, Tax and Benefits*. Accessed online: www.direct.gov.uk/MoneyTaxAndBenefits/Taxes/fs/en

Doughty, S (2005). "Plans for deferred council tax", *Daily Mail*, 16 August.

Gardiner, J (2005). "Business creation initiative knocked". *Regeneration and Renewal*, 29th July, 3.

Help the Aged and New Policy Institute (2003). *The Impact of Council Tax on Older People's Income*. London: New Policy Institute.

Harrison, F (2004) *Boom Bust: house prices, banking and the depression of 2010*. London: Shepheard-Walwyn.

(HMRC) HM Revenue and Customs (2005) *T15.1 Stamp taxes*. updated September 2005

(HMT) HM Treasury (2005) *Investing for our future: fairness and opportunity for Britain's hard-working families*. Budget 2005. London: HM Treasury.

(HMT) HM Treasury (2004). *Spending Review 2004*. London: HM Treasury.

(HMT and ODPM) HM Treasury and Office of the Deputy Prime Minister (2005). *Housing Policy: an overview*. London: HM Treasury and Office of the Deputy Prime Minister.

(HMT and ONS) HM Treasury and Office for National Statistics (2004). P*ublic Expenditure Statistical Analyses*. London: HM Treasury.

Huhne C (2004). "Why we should follow Pittsburgh". *New Statesman*, 27th September, 38-39.

Kay, J A and King, M (1990). *The British Tax System* 5th edn. Oxford: Oxford University Press.

Lakoff, G (2004). *Don't Think of an Elephant: know your values and frame the debate – the essential guide for progressives*. Vermont: Chelsea Green Publishing.

Land Value Taxation Campaign (2002). *What is Land Value Taxation?* Accessed online: www.landvaluetax.org.uk/whatis.htm.

Lyons Inquiry (2004). *Lyons Inquiry into Local Government Funding*. Accessed online: www.lyonsinquiry.org.uk.

Maxwell, D (2004). *Fair Dues: Towards a More Progressive Inheritance Tax*. London: ippr.

Monk, S; Crook, T; Lister, D; Rowley, S; Short, C and Whitehead, C (2005). *Land and Finance for Affordable Housing: the complementary roles of Social Housing Grant and the provision of affordable housing through the planning system*. York: Joseph Rowntree Foundation.

National Statistics (2005). T*he Effects of Taxes and Benefits on Household Income, 2003-04*. London: National Statistics.

(ODPM) Office of the Deputy Prime Minister (2004). *Balance of Funding Review – Report*. London: Office of the Deputy Prime Minister

(ODPM) Office of the Deputy Prime Minister (2005). *Sustainable Communities: homes for all. A Five Year Plan from the Office of the Deputy Prime Minister*. London: Office of the Deputy Prime Minister

Planning Resource (2005). *New development tax for Milton Keynes growth. Planning Resource*, 14th April. Accessed online: www.planning.haynet.com.

Porter, R (2005). "Prezza backs land tax". *Daily Express*, 14th July, pg 20.

Riley, D (2001). *Taken for a Ride: trains, taxpayers and the Treasury*. Middlesex: Centre for Land Policy Studies.

Roger Tym and Partners (2005). *The Cost & Funding of Growth in South East England*. London: Roger Tym and Partners.

(South East Commission) Commission on Sustainable Development in the South East (2005). *Commission on Sustainable Development in the South East Final Report*. London: ippr

Travers, T (2005). "Freedom is a must for sustainable communities to work". *Local Government Chronicle*, 23rd June, pg 7.

(VOA) Valuation Office Agency (2005). *Business Rates: an introduction*. Accessed online: www.voa.gov.uk/publications/public_fact_sheets/-introduction_bus_rates.pdf.

Vigor, A and Robinson, P (2005). *Meeting Housing Need in the South East*. Accessed online: www.ippr.org.uk/ecomm/files/housing_paper.pdf.

Weaver, M (2005). Plan to tax property developers revealed. *The Guardian*, 13th July. Accessed online: www.society.guardian.co.uk/publicfinances/story-/0,12671,1527881,00.html.

2 The politics of land tax - then and now

Iain McLean, Professor of Politics, University of Oxford[3]

Introduction

Land taxation is rising rapidly up the UK political agenda. The 2005 General Election showed that Council Tax was a deadly issue. Both opposition parties made irresponsible promises to reduce the tax on real estate, and the then local government minister Nick Raynsford joined the auction by promising not to create new upper bands for Council Tax. Now that the election is over, more responsible thoughts may return. The Lyons Inquiry of local taxation will report in December 2005. The present signs are that it may take taxation of land values seriously – if only because all the other options look unattractive on closer inspection. This paper aims to show that land value tax has positive merit. The next section, Classical arguments: Paine, Ricardo, Henry George and Lloyd George traces the normative argument for land value tax in the words of its most persuasive proponents since Tom Paine. It shows how some of the classical arguments for inheritance tax also work as arguments for a land tax. Section 3, Could a land tax work? addresses the issues of practicability, and of winners and losers.

Classical arguments: Paine, Ricardo, Henry George and Lloyd George

Tom Paine

Tom Paine was not the first land taxer. The French 'Physiocrats', a school founded by the physician François Quesnay in the 1750s, believed that land was the sole source of wealth and the only proper base for taxation. The Physiocrats were part of the scientific Enlightenment. Adam Smith describes Physiocrat single-tax economics as 'a system which never has done, and probably never will do any harm in any part of the world' – a nice example of Smithian irony (Smith 1776/1976 p. 663; IV: ix). Actually, it has done harm, because land taxers have been labelled as 'single-taxers' and caricatured as cranks.

Our story therefore starts with a rougher but more persuasive thinker, Tom Paine (1737-1809). The subtitle of his *Agrarian Justice* (1797) demonstrates his remarkably modern-sounding concerns:

---

3 This paper is based on "Land Tax: Options for Reform", in The Citizen's Stake (2006, forthcoming) edited by Will Paxton and Stuart White with Dominic Maxwell. Many thanks to the Policy Press for permission to use it.

AGRARIAN JUSTICE,/OPPOSED TO/AGRARIAN LAW/AND TO/AGRARIAN MONOPOLY/BEING A PLAN FOR MELIORATING THE CONDITION OF MAN, BY CREATING IN EVERY NATION A NATIONAL FUND,

To pay to every Person, when arrived at the Age of TWENTY-ONE YEARS, the Sum of FIFTEEN POUNDS Sterling, to enable HIM or HER to begin the World!

And also,

Ten pounds Sterling per Annum during life to every Person now living of the Age of FIFTY YEARS, and to all others when they shall arrive at that Age, to enable them to live in Old Age without Wretchedness, and go decently out of the World (Paine, 1797/1995: 409).

Paine's political thought is equally rooted in the American and the French Enlightenments and reflects his friendship with the stellar figures of each, Thomas Jefferson and the Marquis de Condorcet. *Agrarian Justice* is addressed to the Directory which then governed France. Paine takes from John Locke the basic idea that in the state of nature all property is held in common. But he goes further:

Man, in a natural state, subsisting by hunting, requires ten times the quantity of land to range over, to procure himself sustenance, than would support him in a civilized state, where the earth is cultivated.... [B]ut it is nevertheless true, that it is the value of the improvement only, and not the earth itself, that is individual property. Every proprietor therefore of cultivated land, owes to the community a ground rent... and it is from this ground rent that the fund proposed in this plan is to issue (Paine, 1797/1995: 417-8).

Paine calculates national wealth and mortality rates, using UK data from Prime Minister Pitt the Younger's Budget of 1796, plus some (heroic) actuarial assumptions about life expectancy. He assumes life expectancy of 30 more years at age 21, the age at which each would get his or her £15 citizen's stake to begin the world. He notes that fewer than half the babies born reach that age. He therefore assumes that 1/30 of those over 21 die in any one year, and therefore that 1/30 of the (privately-held) assets in the economy change hands each year. The same proportion of national wealth is therefore available annually for redistribution, which Paine proposes to do by a 10% inheritance tax. He calculates that this would suffice both for his £15 endowment and his old age pensions.

There are three components to Paine's argument. Using modern terminology:

1 ***Land was originally an unowned common-pool resource. It is therefore legitimate for the community to tax it***. This argument itself comes in two varieties. One comes direct from Locke's *Second Treatise of Government,* Chapter V on property. Paine's argument that hunter-gatherers, lacking private property, remain poor echoes Locke (*2nd Treatise,* 41). It was also used, perhaps independently, by Condorcet, whose *Esquisse* ('Sketch of a history of the progress of the human mind' – Condorcet 1795/1988) had been published posthumously shortly before Agrarian Justice. The second, but weaker, justification of land tax came from the Physiocrats' belief that ultimately land was the sole source of wealth.

2 ***There is no natural right to bequeath, nor to inherit. Inheritance tax is therefore morally justified***. Land reform was a common theme of the French and American Enlightenments. Reformers in both countries tried to sweep away the old rules of inheritance. The most eloquent was Thomas Jefferson. In a letter to James Madison, written from Paris in 1789, Jefferson wrote:

> *The question Whether one generation of men has a right to bind another, seems never to have been started either on this or our side of the water.... I set out on this ground which I suppose to be self evident, "that the earth belongs in usufruct to the living"; that the dead have neither powers nor rights over it.... Then no man can by natural right oblige the lands he occupied, or the persons who succeed him in that occupation, to the paiment of debts contracted by him. For if he could, he might during his own life, eat up the usufruct of the lands for several generations to come, and then the lands would belong to the dead, and not to the living, which would be the reverse of our principle. What is true of every member of the society individually, is true of them all collectively, since the rights of the whole can be no more than the sum of the rights of individuals (Thomas Jefferson to James Madison, 06.09.1789, in Jefferson, 1999: 593).*

Jefferson calculated that the probability that one of any pair of contractors has died reaches 0.5 somewhere between 19 and 20 years after the date of the contract. As the dead cannot bind the living, all contracts should be void after 19 years (McLean and Hewitt, 1994: 58-9). Like other ideas floating around the Condorcet-Jefferson-Paine connection, it was grounded in the new science of applied probability and the new data from actuarial life tables, which fascinated all three thinkers.

3 ***It is legitimate to levy capital taxes on personal as well as real property.***

> *Personal property is the effect of Society; and it is as impossible for an individual to acquire personal property without the aid of Society, as it is for him to make land originally. Separate an individual from society, and give him*

an island or a continent to possess, and he cannot acquire personal property (Paine, 1797/1995: 428).

In other words, personal property can only exist because of the norms and conventions of law and exchange. These are social constructs. Therefore the society which makes them possible has a right to tax them. This argument was used in the UK between 1909 and 1914. It is time to revisit it.

David Ricardo

David Ricardo (1772-1823) formalised, and vastly improved, the arguments of the Physiocrats.

Rent is that portion of the produce of the earth, which is paid to the landlord for the use of the original and indestructible powers of the soil. It is often, however, confounded with the interest and profit of capital, and, in popular language, the term is applied to whatever is annually paid by a farmer to his landlord. If, of two adjoining farms of the same extent, and of the same natural fertility, one had all the conveniences of farming buildings, and, besides, were properly drained and manured, and advantageously divided by hedges, fences and walls, while the other had none of these advantages, more remuneration would naturally be paid for the use of one, than for the use of the other; yet in both cases this remuneration would be called rent. But it is evident, that a portion only of the money annually to be paid for the improved farm, would be given for the original and indestructible powers of the soil; the other portion would be paid for the use of the capital which had been employed in ameliorating the quality of the land, and in erecting such buildings as were necessary to secure and preserve the produce (Ricardo, 1817).

Ricardo was the founder of classical economics. But he was also the godfather of its illegitimate children, Marxian and Georgeite economics. Rent invariably proceeds from the employment of an additional quantity of labour with a proportionally less return, argues Ricardo later in the same chapter:

The rise of rent is always the effect of the increasing wealth of the country, and of the difficulty of providing food for its augmented population. It is a symptom, but it is never a cause of wealth; for wealth often increases most rapidly while rent is either stationary, or even falling. Rent increases most rapidly, as the disposable land decreases in its productive powers. Wealth increases most rapidly in those countries where the disposable land is most fertile, where importation is least restricted, and where through agricultural improvements, productions can be multiplied without any increase in the proportional quantity of labour, and where consequently the progress of rent is slow (ibid.).

Therefore, for Ricardo, land rents were inherently monopolistic. Landowners as landowners contributed nothing, unlike suppliers of capital and of labour, to the productive economy, and their rents rose inversely with prosperity. An abundant factor of production commands a zero rent. Under perfect competition, rents from capital and labour will tend to zero. Ricardian rents from land will not, because land is inherently scarce.

Henry George and David Lloyd George

Ricardo's theory of rent helped to mobilise the Anti-Corn Law League and the Repeal of the Corn Laws in 1846. But the logical implications of Ricardian rent theory for taxation were not drawn until two generations later. In 1871, Henry George (1839-97) was a journalist in a San Francisco which was growing with astonishing speed thanks to the Gold Rush. Land and railroad owners were making conspicuous monopoly profits. The Central Pacific Rail Road controlled all overland traffic from the East, and its proprietors had extracted Ricardian monopoly rents from the US people, via the US Congress, which had empowered them to build the western end of the intercontinental railroad. In *Progress and Poverty* (George, 1879/[1911]), Henry George argued for the abolition of private property in land. However, *Progress and Poverty* does not proceed with a programme of land nationalization, but rather of land taxation. In a chapter headed "The proposition tried by the canons of taxation", George observes:

The best tax by which the public revenues can be raised is evidently that which will closest conform to the following conditions:

1. *That it bear as lightly as possible upon production – so as least to check the increase of the general fund from which taxes must be paid and the community maintained.*

2. *That it be easily and cheaply collected, and fall as directly as may be upon the ultimate payers – so as to take from the people as little as possible in addition to what it yields the government.*

3. *That it be certain – so as to give the least opportunity for tyranny or corruption on the part of officials, and the least temptation to law-breaking and evasion on the part of the taxpayers.*

4. *That it bear equally – so as to give no citizen an advantage or put any at a disadvantage, as compared to others (George, 1879/[1911]: 290).*

This comes directly from Adam Smith (cf. Smith, 1776/1976: 825-7; V.ii.b). It goes beyond, and is detachable from, the Ricardian theory of rent. George later became closely identified with what his followers have always called "the single tax" (Barker, 1955: 509). They argued, not just that land should be taxed, but that only land should be taxed. This was to regress from Ricardo to the Physiocrats, and has unfortunately given the followers of Henry George a cranky reputation.

George had far more influence on the British and American left than did Karl Marx (see, e.g., Pelling, 1965: 10). He visited Ireland and Britain during the Irish land campaign and British agricultural depression in 1881-2 and 1884-5. His ideas spread throughout the British left: to the Liberal, Labour, and Irish parties. They culminated in Lloyd George's budgets of 1909 and 1914. In 1909, Lloyd George introduced taxation of land values, to be implemented when a land valuation register was ready. It was this aspect of the budget that most inflamed the dukes and that provoked Lloyd George's finest oratory. Anticipating (and helping to provoke) the House of Lords' rejection of the 1909 Budget, Lloyd George said:

The question will be asked "Should 500 men, ordinary men chosen accidentally from among the unemployed, override the judgment – the deliberate judgment – of millions of people who are engaged in the industry which makes the wealth of the country?" That is one question. Another will be, who ordained that a few should have the land of Britain as a perquisite; who made 10,000 people owners of the soil, and the rest of us trespassers in the land of our birth[?]... These are the questions that will be asked. The answers are charged with peril for the order of things the Peers represent; but they are fraught with rare and refreshing fruit for the parched lips of the multitude (Newcastle upon Tyne, October 10, 1909, quoted by Jenkins, 1968: 94).

These arguments descend from Paine, Ricardo, and Henry George. Lloyd George was not alone. In reading the speech below, note not only who first said it in 1909, but who revived it in 2003.

Roads are made, streets are made, services are improved, electric light turns night into day, water is brought from reservoirs a hundred miles off in the mountains — and all the while the landlord sits still. Every one of those improvements is effected by the labour and cost of other people and the taxpayers. To not one of those improvements does the land monopolist, as a land monopolist, contribute, and yet by every one of them the value of his land is enhanced. He renders no service to the community, he contributes nothing to the general welfare, he contributes nothing to the process from which his own enrichment is derived (Winston Churchill, 1909, quoted by Barker, 2003: 116).

In 1909 Winston Churchill was a Liberal minister. His Georgeite speech was made in the Commons in defence of his colleague Lloyd George's budget. In 2003 Kate Barker, a business economist and member of the Monetary Policy Committee of the Bank of England, was commissioned by Chancellor Gordon Brown to report on the stickiness of the housing market in the UK and to propose remedies. The analytical chapter from which the quotation comes carries all the implications of an argument in favour of land value tax, although in her recommendations Barker rejects land value tax on the grounds that betterment taxes have always failed. So they have; but betterment taxes are not the same as land taxes. The next section of this paper argues that land tax could work.

The land tax campaign of 1909-14 failed. By 1914 the register of land holdings was still not ready. Lloyd George returned to land taxation in his 1914 Budget, relying on his capacity for brilliant improvisation to work out the details. That had worked when he introduced National Insurance in 1911. This time, on a very complicated subject with powerful vested interests in opposition and no support from his own Treasury officials, Lloyd George failed. The outbreak of World War I put paid to land tax in the UK. Discussion has only restarted in a serious way since 2003. As a sort of echo of the Big Bang of 1909-14, the Liberal Party retained a commitment to "site value rating". In the 2005 election campaign the Liberal Democrats played that down in favour of replacing Council Tax by local income tax (LIT). Charles Kennedy's floundering at his first General Election press conference on who would lose from LIT helped to show that this was a bad idea.

Immediately after the election, Kennedy announced a review of tax policy that was widely taken to be a signal that the Liberal Democrats would ditch LIT again. Labour threw, and the Conservatives promised to throw, Council Tax subsidies in the general direction of 'Devon pensioners'. The Conservatives also promised to abandon the impending revaluation of houses for Council Tax. A government committee (the Balance of Funding Review) and the Commons' ODPM Select Committee both considered land tax in summer 2004 (ODPM, 2004; ODPM Select Committee, 2004). Although they both rejected it, they both engaged (up to a point) with the arguments for it – something that no UK government had done since 1947. The Town & Country Planning Act of that year created a system of rationing land use by planning law, and a system of taxing those who benefited from this created scarcity – i.e. holders of planning permission. The first limb of the Act lives to this day. The second withered and was amputated in 1953. Therefore owners of land with planning permission, or land on which the market believes that planning permission for change of use will be obtained, derive far more economic rent from it than even Ricardo can have imagined possible.

Could land tax work?

Principles

Since Lloyd George, there have been several abortive attempts to tax the windfall gains from planning permission. The standard text on the UK tax system, one of whose authors is now the Governor of the Bank of England, insists that 'the underlying intellectual argument for seeking to tax economic rent retains its force' (Kay and King, 1990: 179). Since 1947, land value in the UK has depended on its planning status. If a field is zoned for agriculture, it is worth a few thousand pounds per hectare. If it is zoned for business, it may be worth millions of pounds per hectare. Land value taxation is efficient (because it does not distort the incentives to develop land) and equitable (because it returns some of the economic rent to the people who created it, namely the local authority and its electors). As Kay and King explain (1990: 181):

Suppose the award of planning permission increases the value of a plot of land from £5000 to £1 million. Then even if the resulting gain were taxed at 90%, the developer would still be better off by almost £100,000 using the land for housing than retaining it for agricultural purposes. Substantial incentives to bring projects forward would remain.

There are two main objections: the expectation that the tax would not be permanent, and the costs of assessment. Property interests have always seen off past attempts at land taxation. This happened not only in 1909 and 1914, but also, as Barker (2003, Box 7.3) notes, in 1947, 1967, 1974, and 1985. On each occasion property owners had an incentive to delay transactions in the hope that their lobbying against the legislation would succeed. On each occasion, they did succeed. The inference to draw is not Barker's inference that land taxation is unfeasible. It is that any tax should be a tax on capital value,[4] not a tax on transactions.

The second objection to land value taxation is the difficulty of assessment. This is less of a problem than it seems. The same difficulty faces both business rates and council tax, the two taxes that land value tax would replace (in whole or in part). Both of these taxes are linked to valuations that rapidly go out of date. Council tax bands are determined by houses' value in 1991. The next Council Tax revaluation in England is due in 2007 and the political flak has already started to fly. A 2005 revaluation in Wales led to more houses moving up than down in relative valuation. This infuriated Welsh taxpayers, but could be robustly regarded as a welcome broadening of the tax base. In the 2005 General Election, the Conservatives promised to delay the 2007 revaluation – a pledge even more irresponsible than the Liberal Democrats' short-lived commitment to LIT.

The base for Uniform Business Rate is revalued only every five years. The more time that elapses between valuations, the more those whose assets have risen in relative value have an incentive to block revaluation. It was

4 Or rental value. True believers in LVT get into a tizzy as to which should be the basis. But the difference is immaterial. The capital value of houses is known, and a rental value can be deduced from it. The rental value of business premises is known, and a capital value can be deduced from it.

just such a revolt against rating revaluation in the 1980s that led to the poll tax disaster.

Enough houses change hands every year that the capital value of every house in the land could be calculated annually. Estate agents do it all the time, in their ordinary business. Therefore there is no reason why a public sector valuer (the existing Valuation service or a successor) could not do the same. Commercial and industrial property changes hands less often, so that annual valuation of every parcel of land may not be feasible. But this is not an insuperable objection. At worst a government could stick with the existing five-yearly revaluation, which could be updated whenever a sale took place. A good deal of detailed work would be required in order to calculate the correct taxation basis when land is leased rather than sold (and any prospect of a land value tax would give owners an incentive to sell leases rather than freeholds). So land value taxation is not an option for tomorrow. But it could be an attractive option for 2009, the centenary year of the People's Budget. A National Land and Property Gazetteer is already being constructed, by uniting databases from the Ordnance Survey, the Royal Mail, and local and central government. In principle it can identify every taxable hereditament in the UK. And it is not a snooper's charter, because it contains information only about places, not about people.

A third objection, currently politically salient, is that any property tax including land tax penalises the "asset-rich but cash-poor" – who in current debate are characterised as "Devon pensioners". The first, robust, answer, is that Devon pensioners should face the real opportunity cost of continuing to live in large houses, and they have the options of taking in lodgers or trading down to smaller houses. A softer answer is that the tax liability on a freehold house could be deferred if the householder cannot pay, and become a charge on the estate when the house is sold. Local authorities would be able to borrow against this debt owed to them, and would therefore not be deprived of a cash flow.

Land tax would be a tax on land value, or more strictly on the economic rent deriving from land value. Therefore it should be levied at a zero rate at land that has no value above baseline agricultural use – John Muellbauer has proposed elsewhere a zero rate band up to £10,000/hectare. Above that, it would not depend on whether land had a planning permission, but on whether the market believed that it would get planning permission – thus it would catch speculative appreciation in land values on urban fringes. A fourth objection is therefore that if it is partly a local tax (which on balance I think it should be), land tax gives cash-strapped councillors an incentive to permit sprawling developments and US-like malls from which the 1947 system protects the UK. The answer to that objection is that councils, like Devon pensioners, should face the true opportunity cost of their decisions. And so should the people they represent. Refusing development comes at a cost which at present local citizens do not bear. They should face the open choice: *Permit development and face lower local tax rates, or refuse it and face higher local tax rates*. The ballot box should decide.

This argument works both ways. If an authority proposes a development that reduces land values – say an incinerator or a tannery next to a housing estate – it is right that those who take the decision should face the true costs in a reduced land tax income flow.

Finally, as a land tax would tax Ricardian rents, it must be a tax on *that portion of the produce of the earth, which is paid to the landlord for the use of the original and indestructible powers of the soil,* to repeat Ricardo's words. Therefore it is a tax on land, not on the structures that sit on the land. This means that a future valuation regime would have to separate those two. In the case of houses, that is both fair and uncomplicated. Every Sunday the papers tell you what improvements add value to your house and what do not. In the case of commercial and industrial premises, it is admittedly more complicated.

To get a feeling for the magnitudes involved, Table 1 reproduces the lat-

Table 1: UK government: Current receipts (£ billion)

	Outturn 2003-04	Estimate 2004-05	Projection 2005-06
Inland Revenue			
Income tax (gross of tax credits)	118.4	126.8	138.1
National Insurance contributions	72.5	77.9	82.6
Corporation tax	28.6	34.1	43.7
Tax credits	-5.0	-4.6	-4.4
Petroleum revenue tax	1.2	1.3	1.5
Capital gains tax	2.2	2.3	3.0
Inheritance tax	2.5	2.9	3.4
Stamp duties	7.5	8.9	9.7
Total Inland Revenue (net of tax credits)	228.0	249.6	277.5
Customs and Excise			
Value added tax	69.1	72.3	76.3
Fuel duties	22.8	23.5	24.6
Other	23.8	24.6	25.6
Total Customs and Excise	115.7	120.4	126.5
Vehicle excise duties	4.8	4.8	5.1
Business rates	18.3	19.0	19.4
Council tax	18.8	19.8	20.9
Other taxes and royalties	11.2	12.0	12.4
Net taxes and National Insurance contributions	396.8	425.6	461.9
Other receipts and adjustments	22.1	24.1	24.8
Current receipts	418.9	449.7	486.7

Source: Budget 2005, Financial Statement & Budget Report (London: HM Treasury 2005), Table C8

est (Budget 2005) UK official estimates of the current yield of each main tax, including all taxes that land value tax could replace or supplement. Table 1 shows that tax proceeds on capital transactions are low, whereas even under the existing regime tax proceeds on (purported) land values are much higher. In the former class, IHT, Capital Gains Tax, and Stamp Duty jointly yielded £12.2 bn (3% of receipts) in 2003-04. In the latter class, business rates and council tax jointly yielded £37.1 bn (9 per cent of receipts). Neither class of taxation comes anywhere near capturing the windfall gains of which Winston Churchill spoke in 1909, nor anywhere near recouping any of them for the public sector. Consider the case of transport improvements, for example. The Jubilee Line Extension, from Green Park to Stratford, was commissioned in the early 1990s for completion in time for the opening of the Millennium Dome, at its North Greenwich station. Because it was common knowledge that government credibility depended on its opening by 1 January 2000, suppliers of both capital and labour to the project extracted huge rents, and its costs overran hugely (for that and other reasons). Nevertheless, studies by Transport for London show that, even at the bloated costs incurred, the Jubilee Line Extension could very easily have been financed by a land tax. Property values adjacent to its stations rose hugely – by £2.8 bn at Southwark and Canary Wharf alone. Even at stations not on the Extension, property values rose by more than the general rate. People living near Stanmore station at the other end of the line had a new means of getting conveniently to other parts of London – not only to the Dome, but also to useful places such as Southwark and Canary Wharf. However, the UK government not only failed to extract any tax revenues from the uplift at Canary Wharf, it actually offered the area an undeserved and instantly capitalised tax break in the shape of stamp duty exemption for sales of commercial properties in "deprived wards". This tax break was hastily withdrawn in Budget 2005.

Transport improvements cost money. The commonest source of land value gain, however, costs nothing except staff wages: namely, planning permissions for changes from a low-rent land use (such as agriculture) to a high-rent use (such as an out of town shopping centre). Here, the economic rent is created because planning law, for basically benign reasons, deliberately creates a scarcity. Left to themselves, market forces might produce a suburban Britain that looks like suburban America. Almost nobody at any point of the political spectrum wants that. Therefore, since 1947, there have been tight zoning restrictions on land-use planning in the UK. However, there has been too much sentiment and too little hard-headedness about the economic and social issues involved in the 1947 regime, which is still in place. The 1947 regime is very indulgent to farmers, which was appropriate after the blockades and food shortages of both World

Wars, but no longer is. It produced socially desirable policies such as Green Belts by command-and-control, not by price signals. And, although nobody wants an unregulated market in land use, a regulated market would far outperform the present command-and-control regime.

At present the UK has a raft of bad land taxes. They include Council Tax; business rates; Stamp Duty; IHT and CGT to the extent that they catch increases in land values (which is not much, as those who benefit can pay for sophisticated tax advice); and, probably worst of all, Section 106 Agreements. The last are agreements between a developer and a locally authority whereby the developer agrees to contribute to some socially desired outcome (such as subsidising social housing or urban transport) in return for the grant of planning permission. S.106 agreements are the worst sort of disguised taxation. They are extremely costly to both developers and local authorities; and the gains they produce are in no way commensurate to the cost. A simple auction of planning permissions would do far better. A tax levied on land value (and not on transactions, as IHT, CGT, Stamp Duty, and the abortive 1947, 1967, and 1974 land taxes all were) would be better yet.

Political Prospects

Land value tax (LVT) could replace Council Tax, business rates, or both. It could (and probably should) also replace Stamp Duty and Inheritance Tax – Table 1 shows that these are small beer, so their abolition would be politically popular and help assuage the losers from a switch to land value taxation. But the arguments are different for houses (Council Tax) and businesses (Business Rates, strictly National Non-Domestic Rate, NNDR). On balance I am too much of a coward to recommend switching from Council Tax (CT) to LVT on domestic property, but I am brave enough to recommend switching from NNDR to LVT on non-domestic property.

Simulations of the effect of switching to LVT in a sample suburban area show that if total yield were held equal to the present joint yield of CT and NNDR, but LVT were levied at a uniform rate in the £ on all land, there would be a huge swing of the tax burden from businesses to houses. This is obviously a political non-starter, so it is necessary to add the constraint that in its first year LVT on business should yield the same as NNDR and LVT on houses the same as CT. This implies, of course, that the rate in the £ of LVT would be much lower on houses than on businesses. There would be some evasion issues, although perhaps no greater than at present with houses being used, but not taxed, as business premises.

On houses, there would be many losers. That is inevitable from any reform of CT, as it is notoriously regressive. The losses among pensioners and other low-income high-wealth taxpayers could be softened by a deferment scheme, and by better integration of CT Benefit – to become LVT

Benefit – with the rest of the tax and benefits system. And it must be remembered that low-income high-wealth householders are a tiny (maybe 2%), however noisy, proportion of all householders. A more serious problem is that LVT might become a tax on gardens, and hence on biodiversity, which is greater in suburban gardens than out on the prairie. House owners with large plots would be tempted to sell off part of their plot for a new house, and the local authority (which benefits from the increased tax take) might agree.

The new government will have to annoy the rich whatever it does – even if it makes the minimum acceptable change by rebanding Council Tax at the top, which it is presumably free to do, now that Mr Raynsford is no longer a minister and his promise not to create new upper bands for Council Tax has gone with him. Maybe, however, LVT on houses is just a move too far. That is not for me to judge.

On businesses, there are the technical (and non-trivial) issues of the formal incidence of taxation and apportionment of liability among multiple occupiers of each taxable hereditament. But LVT has the huge advantage already mentioned, of capturing betterment value. It also encourages land to be brought into the best use, and therefore is an ideal solution to the underuse of brownfield land. Operational land – roads, railway track, sewage farms -should be exempt, but otherwise public-sector occupiers of land should be liable to taxation at the same rate as private-sector occupiers. This should help to dislodge, for instance, the Department of Health and the Ministry of Defence – even, dare I suggest, the Duchy of Cornwall? – from land that has a more profitable use. The main losers from a switch from NNDR to LVT would be land-extensive businesses. Of these, most farms would be exempt if the suggested £10,000/hectare lower threshold was applied. And those that were not exempt would be deservedly in the tax net, because either they yielded exceptionally high farm income (maybe because of CAP subsidies), or the market regarded them as having development potential, which should be taxed. Land-extensive mineral extraction presents no problem. Golf courses maybe do. There should be a public-benefit exemption from LVT for publicly-accessible open space. Privately-owned golf courses (and stately homes, and other extensive land users) could then qualify for the exemption if the public had sufficient access to them.

Finally, although there is a case (explored by John Muellbauer in Chapter 3) for regarding land taxation as a tool for central government, because of its role as an automatic stabiliser (bubble-pricker), I prefer to regard it as the most appropriate base for local taxation. Land does not move and cannot be hidden. It is more robust than 1991 house values as a tax base. It would be both a more equitable and – importantly – a more efficient tax base for local authorities, for it would encourage them to make best use of the land on their patch, and consider the true opportunity cost of failing to take land-use decisions.

Conclusion: Implementing Paine

Tom Paine's argument is sound. Landowners accrue monopoly rents, which society has a right to tax for two reasons: first, that Ricardian rents should be taxed even if they arise without policy intervention; second, that policy interventions confer windfall gains, which it is appropriate for the community to tax. Paine assumed that the right tax was inheritance tax, but this can be queried. It is unpopular; it is a tax on transactions, not on wealth; it is easy to evade. Death is an involuntary transaction, unlike those that trigger liability to CGT and Stamp Duty – but a taxpayer with foresight can give away assets before death in order to mitigate IHT liability. Henry George succinctly gives the reasons why land tax is both more efficient and more equitable. It is efficient because it is hard to evade and because it minimally distorts economic activity. It would improve UK housing supply, as Barker's evidence shows, even though she shies away from that conclusion herself.

Admittedly, its transaction costs are high, but these have to be incurred already for the existing tax regime of council tax and business rates. Also, the formal incidence of land tax lies on landowners, whereas the formal incidence of business rates lies on occupiers. In economic theory, this difference matters not at all, for the reasons given by Kay and King (1990). In practice it would create considerable problems of transition, because UK business premises are typically let on long leases with upward-only rent reviews. A tax change that transferred liability from occupiers to freeholders would in the long run be neutral because rent agreements would change to accommodate it. But there would have to be some (perhaps messy) transitional arrangements.

The present tax regime suppresses economic activity (S.106 agreements) and encourages bubbles (Council Tax). Land tax could yield more while costing less. Policymakers have an opportunity to implement Tom Paine's dream. Which is also the dream of David Ricardo, Henry George, and Lloyd George. What better way than that could there be to mark the centenary of the People's Budget in 2009?

In the interim, policymakers could do much to prepare the way. They could make Council Tax less regressive in its dying years by rebanding at the top and at the bottom, as evidence to the Balance of Funding Review, and the ODPM Select Committee, both recommended in July 2004. They could announce at the revaluation in 2007 (which will provoke huge protests from those whose property has risen in value) that the government is committed to introducing a fairer system from 2009, and throw in the abolition of IHT and domestic Stamp Duty as sweeteners. They could scrap the over-complicated schemes that either fail to achieve what they set out to, or achieve the opposite. Stamp Duty exemption for non-domestic property transactions in "deprived" areas such as Canary Wharf has already gone. Section 106 Agreements and the Local Authority Business Growth Incentive scheme could follow it. Radical reform awaits its Lloyd George.

References

Barker, C A (1955). *Henry George*. New York: Oxford University Press.

Barker, K (2003). *Review of Housing Supply: securing our future housing needs. Interim Report – Analysis*. London: HM Treasury.

Condorcet, marquis de (1795/1988). *Esquisse d'un tableau historique des progrès de l'esprit humain* ed. A. Pons. Paris: Flammarion.

George, H (1879/[1911]). *Progress and Poverty*. Everyman Edition. London: J.M. Dent.

Jefferson, T (1999). *Jefferson: political writings*. J. Appleby and T. Ball, eds. Cambridge: Cambridge University Press.

Jenkins, R (1968). *Mr Balfour's Poodle* 2nd ed. London: Collins.

Kay, J A and King, M (1990). *The British Tax System* 5th edn. Oxford: Oxford University Press.

McLean, I and Hewitt, F (1994). *Condorcet: foundations of social choice and political theory*. Aldershot: Edward Elgar.

(ODPM) Office of the Deputy Prime Minister (2004). *Balance of Funding Review: report*. London: ODPM.

ODPM Select Committee (2004). **Local Government Revenue: ninth report of session 2003–04** vol. 1: Report. HC 402-I

Paine, T (1797/1995). 'Agrarian Justice'. In *The Political Writings of Thomas Paine*. M. Philp (ed). Oxford: Oxford University Press.

Pelling, H (1965). *Origins of the Labour Party* 2nd ed. London: Oxford University Press.

Ricardo, D (1817). *On the Principles of Political Economy and Taxation*. Accessed online: www.econlib.org/library/Ricardo/ricPContents.html.

Smith, A (1776/1976). *An Inquiry into the Nature and Causes of the Wealth of Nations*. Glasgow edition. Oxford: Oxford University Press.

3 Property Taxation and the Economy

John Muellbauer, Professor of Economics , University of Oxford[5]

Introduction

The ratio of average U.K. house prices to average income or earnings now exceeds previous records. Warnings from the Bank of England and the Financial Services Authority about the potential implications for stability have been frequent in the last two years. Homelessness is on the increase, and housing affordability is again seen as a major problem. There are many similarities with the late 1980s, (Muellbauer 1990). However, the macroeconomic environment is now more benign, partly because of the monetary policy framework introduced in 1997, the greater consistency and predictability of the overall fiscal stance, and lower global inflation risks. HM Treasury (HMT) seems to have taken the view that these reforms, the phasing out of mortgage interest tax relief, and higher Stamp Duty, would eliminate risks of future macroeconomic booms and busts. It has left issues of land use, housing, regional allocation, urban deprivation and regional inequalities largely to the Office of the Deputy Prime Minister (ODPM).

Whether the U.K. should adopt the Euro has been analysed by HMT in the context of the Five Economic Tests, with unprecedented thoroughness. This has refocused policy attention on macroeconomic stability, resource allocation, and distributional issues associated with housing and land. The Five Economic Tests Assessment concluded: 'the incompatibility of housing structures means the housing market is a high risk factor to the achievement of settled and sustainable convergence' (HM Treasury, 2003a).

In anticipation of 'The Five Tests', in April 2003 the Chancellor asked Kate Barker of the Monetary Policy Committee: 'to conduct a review of issues underlying the lack of supply and responsiveness of housing in the U.K.'. The Interim Report was published in December 2003 and the Final Report and Recommendations in March 2004. These reports add greatly to the debate about housing, land and the economy and set out much valuable information. The recommendations include a radical reform of the

5 This paper is based on an article of the same in the *Economic Journal*, vol. 115, issue 502. Earlier versions of this paper were presented at European Network of Housing Research Conference, Cambridge, July 3rd, the Joseph Rowntree Foundation's 'Easing Shortages of Housing Advisory Group' Meeting, 20th May 2004, the British Property Federation Conference, Brighton April 26th, and a Nuffield College seminar. I am grateful to many individuals for helpful discussions of issues germane to this paper, including Janine Aron, Kate Barker, Ken Bartlett, Richard Best, Alan Evans, Iain McLean, Matthew Oakeshott, Nick Stern, Dave Wetzel, Tony Vickers, Carol Wilcox, Martin Wolf, and other members of the various seminars. Responsibility for views expressed is mine entirely.

planning system with which most economists will sympathise, controversial and, in my view questionable, new development taxes and a number of other measures.

Simultaneously, the Chancellor asked David Miles to review the mortgage market, especially the preponderance of variable rate mortgages in the U.K. and barriers to the development of fixed rate mortgages, dominant in continental Europe and the U.S.. Miles (2004) argues that the mortgage market is trapped in an unsatisfactory equilibrium: borrowers are ill-informed about longer term mortgage costs and interest rate and other risks. Together with mortgage advisors and lenders, they are excessively focused on the level of initial monthly payments. There is cross-subsidisation from existing customers to new borrowers taking out discounted variable rate mortgages. Such weaknesses clearly increase the risks associated with house price volatility and probably contributed to greater volatility. The Miles Review's recommendations aim to improve advice and information for borrowers, creating a fairer and more transparent pricing structure; and reforms to help lenders fund mortgages and handle risk more cost-effectively.

Finally, as part of the 'Five Economic Tests' documents published in June 2003, HMT published its discussion paper 'Fiscal Stabilisation and EMU'. This noted: 'fiscal instruments impacting on the housing market could help reduce volatility in this sector of the economy (HM Treasury 2003b)'.

Carving up the examination of the issues and possible policy measures into the supply of new housing, the mortgage market and tax clearly had advantages in giving each set of investigators a more tractable problem. However, the property tax issue was not analysed in depth in the HMT discussion paper, though it recurs in ODPM's examination of local taxation and funding issues on which Sir Michael Lyons is to report towards the end of 2005. I will argue that a more holistic view of the economic issues related to housing and land use would probably not have led to the development tax recommendations of the Barker Report. Compartmentalisation is likely also to have compromised the outcomes of the Balance of Funding Review, (ODPM 2004).

In what follows, I will re-examine property and land taxation in a wider economic perspective. With globalisation of international capital markets, the liberalisation of domestic credit markets, and the widely acknowledged pro-cyclicality of the capital adequacy requirements agreed under the Basel II Accords, these issues are now more important than ever.

Some Criteria for Reform of Property Taxation.

There are four main criteria for property tax reform, apart from raising revenue for government. These are: to improve macroeconomic stability; to improve resource allocation; to lower economic inequality and social exclusion; and to support concerns over the environment, sustainability and other social values.[6] These are looked at in more detail below.

Reforms should also help to simplify the tax system. They need to be phased in gradually to avoid disrupting long-term contracts and causing too sharp shifts in expectations. They need to be co-ordinated with essential reforms of the land-use planning system, which, in its present form, leads to resource misallocations that can only be described as grotesque.[7] Finally, property tax reforms need to be politically feasible in a society, where, although each adult citizen has an equal vote, the distribution of power and influence remain very unequal.

Macroeconomic Stability.

Since Irving Fisher's 1933 'debt deflation' theory of depressions, economists have been much concerned with the way credit market imperfections impact macroeconomic fluctuations – the 'financial accelerator' (Bernanke and Blinder, 1992; and Bernanke, Gertler, and Gilchrist, 1996, 1999). Asset price fluctuations transmitted to economic activity via the financial accelerator operate for both firms and households. The collateral role of property allows credit expansion and additional spending in upswings, thus fuelling booms. Asset price falls e.g., in bubble collapses, can worsen downturns via a credit crunch, or even lead to Japanese-style problems of bad debts weighing down the banking system for prolonged periods. In the U.K., the financial accelerator for households is even more important than that for firms and has become more pronounced since the credit market liberalisation that began in 1980 (Fernandez-Corugedo and Muellbauer, 2004). The higher sensitivity of U.K. consumption to housing wealth since 1980, as well as the greater sensitivity of housing wealth to short-term interest rates compared with Eurozone economies (Maclennan *et al* 1998; 2000), was confirmed by HMT's study on house prices and consumption. It played a significant role in the negative outcome of the Five Economic Tests.

Further feedbacks in the financial accelerator occur via the asset base of banks. Many observers take the view that the Basel II Accords on capital adequacy ratios of banks (due to replace the original 1988 accords in 2006) are likely to increase the 'pro-cyclicality' of these ratios, (see Danielsson, 2003; Goodhart, Hofmann and Segoviano, 2004; and Taylor and Goodhart, 2004; the latter for a thorough review of the issues and literature). This increases the need for stronger stabilisers of asset prices and hence the economy, such as property taxes.

---

6 It can be argued that these criteria were all considered in the Barker Review of the supply of new housing.

7 See Cheshire and Sheppard (2004).

There is also some evidence that house prices and business rents play a role in wage and price determination. Cameron and Muellbauer (2001) find, in the context of a model to explain the evolution of relative earnings of men in British regions relative to the national average, that relative house prices in the previous year have significant positive effects.[8] Bowdler (2003) finds a lag of about 2.5 years between rents and consumer price inflation, though other influences on inflation are more important. This could operate via 5-year lease contracts with upward-only rent reviews.

Concern with macroeconomic stability is not an arcane academic curiosum but is relevant to all stake-holders in the property sector. The industry suffered disproportionately in the early 1990s U.K. slump, following the excesses of the late 1980s. The bankruptcies of many house-builders, the collapse of training schemes, plant closures in the building supply industry, and unemployment of workers in the industry, almost certainly contributed to the weak supply response in the subsequent up-turn (see Barker Interim Review 2003, Chapter 6).

Resource Allocation

Regional employment inequality, urban deprivation, and the 'low demand' inner city areas are all symptoms of inefficiency in the allocation of resources, as well as of inequality and social exclusion. Huge differences exist between economic returns of land in different uses, which cannot be justified as 'benefits to the wider community'. Though some of the most extreme are due more to the planning system than the tax system,[9] I shall argue that serious distortions come from the current tax system. A closely-related resource allocation issue is the under-provision of housing, which the Barker Review sees as a major inefficiency. Taxation (as well as planning reform) can increase new housing supply and improve the allocation of the existing stocks of housing and land. There is also need for approximate tenure neutrality in the tax system, so that certain types of contracts are not arbitrarily discriminated against. Finally, since different types of taxes have different incentive effects on economic activity, a balance of taxation that puts more weight on taxes with smaller deadweight losses is to be preferred.

---

8 At the regional as well as national level, earnings also have far stronger and immediate effects on house prices, see Muellbauer and Murphy (1994, 1997).

9 Consider the case of an industrial-scale sugar beet farm in a relatively featureless East Anglian landscape, the hedgerows having been removed decades ago. Heavily subsidised by U.K. and E.U. tax-payers, it effectively takes livelihood away from third-world sugar cane farmers. The value of the land in agricultural use, despite the subsidy, as Barker shows, is around one third of one percent of the value of the same land in residential use, and its amenity value is only around one percent of that in residential use. The welfare loss caused by the planning restrictions that bring this about is vast.

Economic Inequality and Social Exclusion

Inequalities between different locations have been mentioned. Homelessness is heightened by the under-provision of housing. Affordability particularly concerns the young without parents both wealthy and generous, as the Barker Review emphasises. Martin Weale[10] has made an important analogy between house price booms and large government deficits as transferring spending power from younger, later generations to current, older ones. Given the concern of economists with intergenerational accounts, and HMT's concern with avoiding large government deficits, this suggests avoidance of such intergenerational inequality as a deliberate policy goal.

Most obviously, however, policy-makers who include reduced economic inequality and social exclusion among their objectives would wish to avoid regressive forms of taxation (such as the current form of Council Tax). While means-tested benefits can be used to ameliorate a regressive tax system, the high marginal tax rates associated with withdrawal of such benefits, have negative incentive and so efficiency effects.

Environment and Sustainable Communities

The Sustainable Communities Plan from the Office of the Deputy Prime Minister (ODPM, 2003) has several key elements: addressing the housing shortage, including affordability and homelessness; and low demand and abandonment; bringing social housing to a decent standard; improving the local environment; and protecting the countryside.

The next section will focus on an aspect of property market dynamics in the U.K., which has implications for stability, regional resource allocation and inequality and social exclusion

The Persistence of Property Returns in the U.K. and Macroeconomic Stability

Returns to property in the UK are both volatile and "persistent" – that is, there is a tendancy for a change in one year to be followed by a broadly similar one in the following year. This is true in the UK whether we look at capital growth on UK commercial property, using data from the Investment Property Databank (IPD), or at the annual rate of growth of house prices (see Muellabuer 2005).

Studies of Anglo-Saxon or Scandinavian-style economies generally relate current house prices to, amongst other factors, the "bubble builder" and the "bubble burster" (Abraham and Hendershott 1996). The "bubble builder" means that current house prices are positively correlated with previous

10 Talk given at HMT's EMU conference, Nov. 2003, and Weale (2003)

house price changes, especially in the UK – so capital gains tend to be followed by further capital gains. The "bubble burster" means that current house prices are negatively correlated with previous house prices relative to previous consumer prices, indicating that if real house prices are 'too high' or 'too low', then house prices will tend to adjust in the appropriate direction. Portfolio managers and analysts often use the terms 'momentum' and 'fundamentals' to describe these two factors. Equations of this type are also termed 'equilibrium correction' models (Engle and Granger, 1987; Hendry, 1995). In equilibrium, the fundamentals of income, interest rates, the housing stock relative to population and other factors determine real house prices (see Muellbauer and Murphy, 1997, for further discussion).[11]

Because property returns are driven by the bubble builder and bubble buster, investors will expect high returns to tend to be followed by high returns, and low returns by low returns. The 'user cost' of property, which subtracts the expected rate of appreciation from the interest and other acquisition and holding costs, can be negative for long periods. Indeed, since 1968, the user cost of housing in the South has been negative 57 percent of the time (Muellbauer 2005: Figure 3). At the same time, the rate of return in housing compared with investing in a building society savings account (defined as house price appreciation, plus imputed rent, minus maintenance and tax costs, all as a fraction of value) has been positive, and often very large, for much of the same period.

Given that these returns are a major factor driving demand for property and so prices, national and local overshooting of property prices is endemic. The next section explains how taxes can reduce this volatility.

The Design of Property Taxation for Stabilisation

The user cost of housing drives demand. A simplified version of the real annual user cost of housing would increase with the nominal interest rate, adjusted for any mortgage interest tax relief; with maintenance and insurance cost as a percentage of value; with transactions cost as a percentage of value; and property tax as a percentage of value; and it would reduce with the expected rate of change of house prices. The effect of all these variables would be increased by the real re-sale value of second-hand house prices.

This simplified version ignores elements such as the proportion of a property's value that is mortgaged, which affects the definition of the inter-

11 These kind of equations can also be used to discuss differences in the information of market participants and differences in views of analysts. Less well informed participants are likely to overstate the 'momentum' or 'bubble builder' components. Analysts differ over the role of the fundamentals. Some, for example, will argue that real but not nominal interest rates play a role, though Meen (1993) has long argued for some role for nominal rates. They therefore obtain different answers to whether and how overvalued the market is.

est rate, and the question of whether the marginal rate or the average rate of property tax is more relevant to the decision being made. It also leaves open the question of what is the most relevant time horizon over which the annual average of transactions costs should be taken. Transactions costs include solicitors' and estate agents' fees and Stamp Duty. There is some evidence that deregulation lowered the costs of the former in the 1980s. Stamp Duty rates have varied considerably, and it is not clear that overall transactions costs are higher now than in the early 1980s, despite higher Stamp Duty in recent years.

But despite simplification, this does demonstrate that the level and design of property taxes has an important causal effect on house prices. In the long-run, the value of a house should equal the value of the stream of "services" it provides, progressively translating the value of future services to their present-value equivalents. More precisely, the value of a house should equal the discounted present value of imputed rent minus maintenance costs minus property taxes.

Using plausible assumptions for maintenance costs (one third of the value of imputed rent), the tax rate (one sixth of imputed rent, here equivalent to one percent of market value), and the real discount rate (six per cent, including a risk premium), abolishing a property tax would increase the value of housing by 33.3 per cent, assuming a zero probability of any future property tax returning. Conversely, going from zero to a tax equivalent to one sixth of imputed rent would lead to a fall in prices of 25 per cent. The assumptions can be varied, but it is hard to avoid concluding that the effects will be substantial. At the time of the abolition of domestic rates, Hughes (1989) and Spencer (1988) argued that this abolition would lead to an appreciation of house prices of the order of 16-22 per cent.[12] In the context of the late 1980s house price and consumption boom, this policy shift at the height of this boom can only be described as macroeconomic folly (see Muellbauer, 1987), quite apart from the regressive distributional effect of the poll tax and its huge collection costs. It was also most unfortunate that property taxes, in the form of Council Tax, were brought back at the trough of the worst U.K. housing recession in 70 years.[13]

The lessons of this episode for how to reduce instability are obvious. Instead of abolishing property tax at the height of booms, it is far better to maintain a tax linked to current or recent house prices throughout the house price cycle and that is thus a constant proportion of capital values. Such a tax will represent an increasing proportion of the value of the services yielded by

---

12 Quang Do and Sirmans (1994) give references to the literature on capitalisation and find empirical evidence from California suggesting a real interest rate of around 4 percent.

13 Given the circumstances of the time, the poll tax element and the weak link of Council Tax with market values had some merit in not destabilising the market further, a merit that had vanished by 1997, in view of the robust upturn in the market.

housing (imputed rent) as house prices rise. Thus, tax as a proportion of the imputed rent will rise and will automatically tend to choke off further appreciation as house prices rise relative to imputed rents and incomes. Furthermore, not only does this dampen appreciation of house prices, but it reduces household cash income and so the feed-backs that run from higher incomes to higher house prices, to higher consumer spending, to higher employment and higher incomes back to house prices. There is also an important expectations mechanism at work: if households extrapolate house price rises into the future, they will anticipate the greater tax burdens this will generate and so make more cautious spending and portfolio decisions.

Conversely, in property market downturns, tax to income ratios will fall and this helps to soften recessions. Denmark has a property tax of around 1 percent in recent years, linked to recent market value, and indeed a progressive element, in that the marginal tax rate is higher for the most expensive properties. Denmark avoided the U.K. macroeconomic imbalances of the post-1996 period (excess house price and consumption growth, trade imbalances, overvalued exchange rate) despite strong income growth, falling unemployment and rising employment levels. Admittedly, Denmark's local land value tax and highly developed, but largely fixed rate mortgage market similar to that of the U.S., are likely to have contributed to this remarkable stability.[14] But the evidence, including the empirical evidence from the Danish Central Bank's own model, suggests an important stabilising role for domestic property taxes. It is no surprise that Denmark has the most effective automatic stabilisers in Europe, according to HMT's fiscal policy study (HM Treasury 2003b).[15]

The macro stabilisation role of property taxes considered so far has been primarily from a demand side perspective. Since the stabilising role via the supply side, and resource allocation issues discussed in the next section overlap, a few brief points will be made here. First, how housing supply affects house prices depends on how responsive the demand for housing is to the real price of housing. The simulations in the Barker Review assume that a one per cent rise in the national housing stock will reduce national house prices by two per cent in the long run, other things being equal.[16] As Barker explains, the more responsive is supply to higher house prices, the less volatile will be

---

14 In Denmark, house price to income ratios did rise quite notably in the late 1990s, with strong economic performance, but much less than in the U.K.

15 Moreover, consumers know that in extreme situations in either direction, tax policy could shift. Indeed, the property tax rate has been lowered in Denmark since 2001, partly in response to popular pressure, but with beneficial macroeconomic effects given the parlous economic conditions in core Eurozone economies to which Denmark has strong economic links.

16 Recent unpublished research by Cameron, Muellbauer and Murphy for ODPM suggests that, in addition to this long run effect, a short-term expansion of housing supply relative to population also has an effect in depressing house prices. This speeds up the adjustment of house prices to new supply.

prices, since higher prices will automatically call forth higher supply, tending to reduce prices. The extent to which supply responds to house price changes, known as the supply elasticity, is currently close to zero in the UK and unlikely to be higher than 0.5 (Meen, 2003). An important aim for Barker is to raise this elasticity, as well as shift supply.

The contribution of property taxes to supply can be divided into the effects on new building, considered by Barker, and the effects on the allocation of the existing stock, outside Barker's brief. Since the existing stock is over 99 percent of total supply, improvements in the utilisation of that stock have potentially large effects on prices. A property tax reform which improves utilisation is likely to have a gradual, but one-off impact on prices through better utilisation, since for many owners and occupiers, altered incentives will affect behaviour only with some delay. However, any permanent effect in increasing the responsiveness of effective supply will reduce house price volatility in the long run.

In general, taxes on property, including land, increase the incentives against keeping property vacant and under-occupied. If taxes are linked with current market values, these incentives are sharpened when property prices rise relative to incomes. For example, with higher taxes induced by higher house prices, households with spare rooms will be more inclined to rent out the space, increasing the effective supply of housing. Without such taxes, the appreciation of housing, and the additional collateral this provides for increased spending, dwarfs the potential income streams that might be generated from renting underutilised space.[17] Indeed, under current conditions, a fall in house prices, associated with a drying up of collateral-backed credit, may even lead to additional supply because of pressure on cash flows, just when such supply is likely to weaken the market further.

The benefits of reform are likely to be large, but hard to quantify precisely in the absence of good data (particularly on square metres of the occupied housing stock linked to the characteristics of the occupiers). But as the existing stock comprises 99% of supply, changing its responsiveness to prices will have an overall effect 99 times greater than changing the responsiveness of new build. If the responsiveness (or "effective elasticity") of the existing stock rose by only 0.03,[18] this would be as beneficial in stabilisation terms as a rise of 3 in the elasticity of new build, which would be regarded as a tremendous success if it were the eventual outcome of the Barker recommendations.

---

17 Over 100,000 homes vacant for over 6 months are on the books of local councils in London, the South East and the East, the areas of greatest demand pressure (Financial Times of May 10th, 2004). Some observers of the buy-to-let purchase surge argue that, while appreciation continues, some properties bought with buy-to-let mortgages are kept empty because of the expense of renting out relative to rents received, and the lack of flexibility in a rapidly moving market, where the owner may wish to sell at short notice.

18 This would mean that a 50 percent rise in real house prices would bring forth a 1.5 percent additional rise in effective supply after the tax reform, compared with before the reform.

Both demand side and supply side arguments thus suggest an important stabilising role for domestic property taxes indexed to house price indices.

Resource Allocation and Tax Design

The second criterion for property tax design examined in Section 2 concerned the efficient allocation of resources. Locations such as Bradford and Liverpool have experienced vicious spirals of economic decline, while housing and the infrastructure elsewhere have been under pressure. While differences in the unemployment rate between regions have narrowed since the 1980s, the same is not true of activity rates (employment/working age population),[19] which reached peaks similar to those of the mid to late 1980s in 2000-1. The low activity rates, particularly for men, in the poorer locations are a clear symptom of resource misallocation. High government expenditures on, for example, Regional Development Agencies, urban renewal projects and expensive schemes e.g., the 'deprived areas' Stamp Duty relief scheme, and 'key worker' housing subsidies could be regarded as another symptom of resource misallocation.[20]

The government's ability to supply public services in the South at reasonable quality and cost, has been hampered by staffing costs given high house prices in the South. This will have contributed to the fact that the price deflator for government services has been rising disproportionately in recent years.

The tendency of user costs to persist is one reason for the exacerbation of the regional inequalities and deprivation. One consequence of 'low demand' housing is often a vicious downward price spiral, where the low demand areas become less desirable when their house prices fall. This increases the total costs of housing, reinforcing their undesirability. Households buying in higher priced areas with rising prices, by contrast, benefit from lower user costs of housing as a result of the price growth.

Similar benefits apply to the land or property costs of businesses, which can prolong investment and employment booms in areas with high relative land prices. This failure of price-signals, measured by user cost, to signal scarcity values during long upswings is likely to exacerbate declines in economic activity in the 'low demand' areas, and over-investment and over-employment in congested successful locations. Cameron and Muellbauer

---

19 See, for example, evidence by Andrew Glyn and Esra Erdem to the Parliamentary Employment Select Committee, Appendix 9 of Minutes of Evidence, April 11, 2000.

20 See the detailed critique of the stamp duty scheme by Lord Oakeshott, speech at the British Property Federation Conference, Brighton 22 April 2004. 'Key worker' subsidy schemes tend to drive up prices further. To the extent that RDAs and urban renewal schemes are compensating for market failure their costs would not, of course, be signs of resource misallocation. However, I argue that distortions in the tax system cause part of the problem these expenditures are designed to rectify and that it would be more efficient to work with the grain of the market by reforming the tax system, rather than relying so heavily on bureaucratic intervention.

(1998) found that expected house price appreciation is a crucial counterweight to high house price to earnings ratios, which otherwise discourage net migration to a high priced region. Our estimates help explain why economic activity continues to be attracted to high priced but prosperous locations.

Another reason for regional inequality and cycles of deprivation lies in the regional and local regressiveness of property taxation. The distortions of the system can be illustrated using Kensington (London) and Kensington (Liverpool). A three-bedroom terraced house costs around 6 times as much in Kensington South (KS) as in Kensington North (KN). The implied land price ratio must be around 12 to 1. KS has one of the lowest Council Tax rates; KN one of the highest in the country, 30 percent higher than KS in 2004-5 for a band D house, though the differentials have narrowed sharply since the late 1990s. Such a terrace will be in band A in KN and in one of the higher bands in KS, say band D. Given the local regressiveness of the tax, the tax on the KN house will be almost as high as that on the KS house, despite it being far cheaper. Seen as a tax on the underlying scarce resource land, the tax rate would, on these assumptions, be around 10 times higher per £ of residential land value in KN. The system is strongly biased against one of the most deprived inner city areas in the country. Research on regional migration (e.g., Hughes and McCormick, 2002), suggests that the unskilled unemployed, who make up the bulk of the unemployed, have a very weak response to house price/earnings differentials. Encouraging the movement of skilled workers, professionals and managers to places like Kensington North, or locations nearby is likely to reduce the local unemployment rate among the unskilled.

From this point of view, the Uniform Business Rate (UBR) is a far less distorting tax. But it is obvious that if the tax base of UBR were shifted towards land (see below), businesses locating in the low land price locations usually associated with economic deprivation would benefit. The environmental benefits of better utilisation of the existing stock of housing and of land should also be noted, especially if it brings new economic activity to old industrial land. Moreover, those concerned with the environmental implications of relaxing planning controls, as recommended by the Barker Review, should be sympathetic to measures which help to control demand. I will now discuss some of these issues further in the context of specific and politically realistic reform proposals.

Tax Reform Proposals

Reform of Council Tax.

I have long argued that the Council Tax is not a sensible tax.[21] It is not indexed to market values (the last valuation was in 1991). It is locally

21 For example, in articles in the Observer and the Guardian in 1997, the Financial Times in 1998, 2000, 2002, and most comprehensively, in Cameron and Muellbauer (2001).

regressive,[22] with a big 'poll tax' element and a zero marginal tax rate for expensive houses; and regionally regressive, with locations with lower house prices tending to have higher Council Tax rates. There was a 50 percent discount until March 2004 for second homes – councils now have discretion to reduce this to a 10 percent discount. There was also an 'empty homes' discount until 2003. And there is no postponement of the tax for pensioners (unlike in Denmark, where pensioners can delay payment until the property is sold) which very much reduces the cash flow burden on those with low cash incomes.

The Liberal Democrats entered the 2005 General Election proposing to replace Council Tax with a local income tax and no property tax whatsoever. In terms of macro-economic stability, abolishing property taxes at the peak of the house price boom, smacks of Mrs. Thatcher's blunder of 1987-9. Reportedly, they are reconsidering their tax proposals after the May 2005 Election.

The analysis of Sections 4 and 5 points to scrapping Council Tax, replacing it with a property tax. The property tax should be national, not local: the central government has better access to the international capital markets and is focused on macroeconomic stability, while stability of revenue is of greater concern to local governments than central government. Property taxes linked to market prices are necessarily more volatile than income or sales taxes, indeed obtaining their automatic stabilising function by rising relative to income in upswings and falling relative to income in downswings. This suggests that they are not ideal as the main source of local revenue. A proportion could be given to local councils to give them a stake in decisions, for example on development, that affect the property tax base. But given its instability, of the order of 75 percent of the revenue from property tax should go to central government. Local income taxes are the most obvious source for the bulk of local authority tax revenue. If central government were to receive 75 percent of domestic property taxes, it would be possible to transfer part of its share of income tax to local government, so that no increase in overall income taxation would occur (unlike the Liberal Democrat proposals). Moreover, as discussed below, the reformed business rate could be divided between local and central government with a larger proportion going to local government to achieve an overall objective of 're-localising' funding.

A sensible rate for a U.K. domestic property tax is probably of the order of half a percent of value, or a little less. Thus, on a £250,000 house, the annual

---

22 It is worth commenting on a supply side aspect of local regressivity. Council Tax creates incentives to combine adjacent small housing units, whether country cottages or flats in a Victorian house, into large single units to lower the tax bill. This not only contradicts planning guidance, which tends to favour smaller units, but goes against the grain of the increasing fraction of small households in the evolving demographic structure. And because units in the rental market tend to be smaller than in the owner-occupied sector, it contributes to the overall tax bias against the rental sector.

tax would be £1,150, not so very different from what many Council Tax payers are currently paying.[23] Note that the Danish rate of one percent is in the context of significant mortgage interest tax relief, abolished in the U.K.

To ease the politics of transition, reform should follow the Danish example of giving pensioners the option to postpone. Together with the redistributive element of this reform, the number of gainers would massively outnumber the losers. Though the latter would be more influential on a per capita basis,[24] it is unlikely they would dominate. If property prices fell, there would be considerable scope for the Bank of England to cut interest rates, helping first time buyers, in particular.

Reform of Business Rates.

The analysis of Sections 4 and 5 also suggests satisfying all four reform criteria by the increased linkage of business taxes to current or recent land values. The following proposal suggests a moderate and politically feasible package and has four main elements. The first is to reform the Uniform Business Rate (UBR), shifting half the basis for valuation away from business assets to land above some minimum value per hectare.[25] The second is to exclude most farmland by e.g., exempting the first £20,000 value per hectare.[26] The third is to permit a payment window e.g., 3-5 years to ease cash flow problems, provided the tax authority has a first claim on the land holding registered at the Land Registry. It might also be worth considering offering the option of payment in land titles, in lieu of cash. Finally, the new Land Value Tax (LVT) regime should be phased in gradually.

In 2002 UBR raised £16bn.[27] It makes sense to raise the LVT target of £8bn a little to compensate for a phased reduction and reform e.g. properly tapering Stamp Duty, which currently raises around £2.5bn from the commercial property sector.

Stamp Duty is a poor tax. It taxes transactions and so is a barrier to mobility both for firms and households. It imposes heavy penalties on sometimes relatively small changes in contractual rights and obligations, from which both sides of the transaction benefit. The 'slab' system makes

---

23 This assumes an allowance for the first £20,000 or so, which would add a mild progressive element to the tax, particularly beneficial in low demand areas and for reducing poverty and unemployment traps. And naturally, benefits analogous to Council Tax benefit, would apply to the poorest households. Given short-term rent contracts in the U.K., and the need for advance warning of the reform, it probably does not matter much whether landlords or tenants pay. The former is administratively cheaper. Net revenue, after tax benefits, is likely to be higher than from current Council Tax at these rates at current property values

24 For example, via the influence of wealthy newspaper proprietors or editors slanting coverage towards their personal self-interests rather than those of their readership.

25 Land value taxation has a long history, aptly summarised by McLean (2004).

26 The exemption would apply only to contiguous parcels of land so that large owners cannot use the acquisition of cheap land to reduce their overall tax liability by averaging.

27 This is about 1.6 percent in 2002 of the values of buildings, civil engineering works, and plant and machinery owned by private corporations.

no sense: arbitrary discontinuities with no economic justification encourage a culture of deceit and avoidance. Indeed, for the commercial sector, largely subject to the maximum rate of 4 percent, much energy has gone into avoidance e.g., by moving partners to transactions offshore. Switching to a simple 2 percent flat rate or a tapered system with a 2 percent maximum for the commercial sector, would likely result in only a moderate revenue loss, requiring little increase, perhaps £1bn, in the LVT component of the UBR to replace lost revenue.

If the LVT component had existed in 2002, generating around £9bn revenue, the tax rate would have been perhaps 2 percent of value.[28] Phasing in over 5 years, would suggest 0.4 percent in the first year, 0.8 percent in the second year, rising to 2 percent in the fifth year and beyond. There would also be an initial delay for a first valuation, giving further scope for businesses to adjust to the new system.

There are numerous benefits of the LVT element in UBR. Governments face increasing difficulties in taxing corporations and there is a pressing need to find alternative tax bases. It yields the highest holding costs of land to owners when and where land prices are highest, so encouraging release of such land when and where it matters most. The Interim Barker Report evidence is that, in these locations and at these times, housing supply elasticities are at their lowest. The tax thus offsets these tendencies which are part of the reason for the overshooting of house prices and the undersupply of housing, reducing the overshooting by making user costs positive for longer, producing improved resource allocation and macroeconomic stability.

The tax falls ultimately upon ownership, and not on development nor on business activity. It captures part of the benefits accruing to land owners from public investment or the private investment of others. It thus underwrites the funding of public investment, since the rise in land values that a worthwhile project engenders will automatically generate a rise in tax revenue to fund the project. This should encourage better public investment decisions not only regarding individual projects, but the scale of such investment. In a sense, it automates the mechanism by which U.S. 'business improvement districts' are used to finance infrastructure. The tax incorporates far better incentives than did the complex and expensive

---

29 According to the National Income and Expenditure Blue Book, buildings and engineering works owned by private corporations in 2002 were valued at around £600bn, with the land value component probably about £300bn. To this can be added the land value of business assets held by unincorporated businesses, unlikely to amount to more than £30bn. However, the tax base would also include unused, but valuable, land currently exempt from UBR. Currently, we lack good estimates of what this might be. If it includes land with planning permission for residential housing and other valuable uses, as well as land with a significant hope value of obtaining such permissions in future, it could add as much as £150bn to the taxable land capacity, even after the £20,000 per hectare tax allowance. On the basis of a £450bn tax base, we would then be thinking of a 2 percent LVT.

Stamp Duty relief for deprived areas (which included Canary Wharf in such a tax exempt area). Businesses locating in deprived areas with low land values would automatically pay substantially lower taxes than at present, and without any administrative intervention, except through the basic valuation and tax collection system. Urban regeneration is likely to be more successful under these circumstances than at present.[29]

Valuation presents some technical difficulties, but none are insuperable. The market price basis is often seen as unfair (e.g. by Barker), where the market value at current planning consents includes a hope value anticipating future changes of this planning consent. Someone owning a couple of acres to keep a horse, near a residential area might then have to pay significant taxes.[30] Even worse, since under current law, anyone can apply for a change in planning consents, a sale may be forced on such an owner by a successful application by another party. A change in the law, requiring the owner's consent for any planning application would deal with this last point. The proposed tax allowance on the per hectare land value and a 3-5 year payment window also help. Another possibility is to permit settlement of tax bills in the form of land rather than in cash.[31] Some would still consider the market value basis unfair under these circumstances even if the owner had experienced considerable capital appreciation or had been wealthy enough to be able to afford the original purchase at a price reflecting hope value. However, fairness can be sometimes in the eye of the beholder.

The alternative of imputing market values given existing consents, excluding any 'hope' element, makes valuation a good deal more complex and, in my view, should be avoided if at all possible. Another alternative of taxing capitalised cash flow, if generally applied, would encourage dereliction. However, when land is already in best use, it can be helpful in solving hard to value cases.

The technical difficulties are now smaller than they have ever been. In recent years major developments have taken place in GIS based mass valuation systems, in the computerisation of the Land Registry, and the development of local gazetteers. Vickers (2000, 2002) has carried out serious research on practical experience with LVT in Pennsylvania, including valuation issues, handling appeals, and the legal framework and has considered in some detail running pilots for introducing LVT into the U.K. Some will argue that land valuation is inherently more difficult than the valuation

29 For a more detailed examination of various LVT design issues, see a fuller version of this paper on housingoutlook.co.uk.

30 To make this concrete, consider a 5 hectare plot which is valued at £50k per hectare because of hope value, instead of £10k per hectare on the basis only of agricultural consent. With a 1 percent tax on the excess of 50k over the 20k exemption, the annual tax would be £1500.

31 In the context of the example in the previous footnote, with a 5 year payment window, this would involve giving up rights to 3 percent of the land holding every 5 years.

problems faced by the Valuation Office in connection with UBR.[32] However, practical experiences in countries such as Denmark, where local taxes have a land value element, and in parts of the U.S., suggests that the obstacles are far from overwhelming.

Nevertheless, it needs to be recognised that land markets are much thinner than residential housing markets. This means that the basis for annual updating of valuations will based on many fewer transactions and so be less reliable than for housing. Currently, valuations for UBR take place every 5 years. In practice, this may well be often enough for the LVT component proposed here. The macro stability arguments for current year valuations for property taxes are also more important for households, where the impact on spending via the expansion of collateral values is likely to be more important than for businesses. A 5 year cycle of valuations also has the advantage that tax revenues are more predictable and stable. It makes sense, therefore, to transfer a large share of this tax revenue to local authorities. Note that even with uniform national business rates, local authorities will then have a strong incentive to make planning and other decisions which will enhance local property values. This reform would help to relocalise taxation.

Proponents of land value taxation suggest that phasing out of UBR entirely while LVT is phased in over, say, ten years, would ultimately be cheaper in administrative costs since only one valuation system is then needed. However, it seems likely that cautious governments would not wish to commit in advance to such a large change before undertaking a smaller scale trial. They may also argue that business rates are long established and to give up a widely accepted revenue source could be risky. Furthermore, business assets as a whole may be more correlated with ability to pay than unimproved land values and to move entirely to the land basis, even with a 3-5 year payment window, could be too radical a shift.

Transition also presents the question of whether the owner or the occupier is liable for the tax. Textbooks tend to suggest this is irrelevant since land taxes will ultimately be shifted to the owner, but credit constraints, myopia and transition can alter this conclusion. Business rates are paid by the occupier and this is reflected in lease-hold arrangements between landlords and tenants. Any unanticipated change in the basis of business rates will disturb existing contractual arrangements. An increase in the land tax relative to the rate implied by the current UBR and not offset by the halving of the tax rate on

32 One leading property expert takes the view that, for example, urban valuations are very hard. To illustrate their complexity, he argues that land values on one side of Oxford St. are 20 percent higher than on the other, and twice as high at one end of the street than the other. However, one hesitates to take this as a sign of difficulty: if one expert can give such precise valuations, one could argue that a professional land agent should be able to be similarly precise.

other business assets will have a negative impact on the cash flows of tenants, which with 5 year upward-only rent reviews cannot quickly be recouped in lower rents. These issues would need to be addressed.

The property tax alternatives to UBR and LVT are not attractive. Estate Duty already exists, and with high property values is yielding buoyant revenues. It has the merit, from the point of view of housing market stability, of encouraging or in some cases, forcing, the sale of the houses of the deceased. However, its stabilisation and efficiency benefits are far weaker than those of market value related property tax as discussed above. The defects of Stamp Duty have been discussed. Capital gains taxes are also a relatively poor form of property taxation. They tend to discourage transactions and the release of under-utilised land or buildings e.g., in expectation of lower future tax rates or offsetting losses. They involve serious complications of roll over relief in practice and indexation. The Barker Review suggests Capital Gains Tax on land sales has had poor revenues and has not been a good way of capturing planning gains in land values. We turn now to the Barker Review proposals in more detail.

The Barker Review proposals

Barker views the existing planning system as a key element in the economic malfunctioning[33] of housing and land markets in the U.K., at both a macro and micro-level. Barker favours its wholesale reform[34] and the introduction of new development taxes – Planning-gain Supplements (PGS) to be awarded on the granting of planning permission – and suggests reform of Section 106 of the 1990 Planning Act. Barker recommends the introduction of real estate investment trusts (REITs) to bring new finance into the rental sector. More new-build social housing should be encouraged, paid for partly by the new development taxes, and registered social landlords reforms undertaken. Affordability criteria should be introduced to guide policy.[35] Subsidies should be extended to develop land that has been derelict for some time.

These recommendations have major implications for the entire property sector, but the strong emphasis on new development taxes is questionable.

33 The McKinsey Global Institute Report (1998) had argued that the land use planning system in the U.K. was a major handicap to U.K. productivity.

34 ODPM have already accepted the proposal to merge Regional Housing Boards and Regional Planning Bodies, and will give the Regional Assemblies ultimate responsibility for planning and meeting housing supply targets, derived from closing the gap between actual and target affordability over some medium- term horizon. An independent advisory unit - a kind of Monetary Policy Committee of new housing supply- is to oversee this process.

35 The ODPM have now adopted this proposal, taking the ratio of the lowest quartile of house prices from the Survey of Mortgage Lenders, to the lowest quartile of individual full-time earnings from the New Earnings Survey and its successor, as the main indicator at the regional and national levels.

Indeed, the Barker Interim Report (2003) itself outlined in detail the failure of previous development taxes.

The narrow remit of the Barker Review, focused on house-building, helps explain the lack of economic analysis of the effects of property taxes in general. New housing annually amounts to just under one percent of housing supply. Taxes on land or property probably have their main effects on the allocation of the existing stocks, and on demand, so consideration of land and property taxes was arguably outside the brief of the Review. Thus, while much-needed Council Tax reform was acknowledged, it was not explored.

The Barker Review's explanation for the lack of responsiveness of new supply to higher house prices is that it is caused mostly by failure of the planning system. Skill shortages are also acknowledged. However, the suggestion, that rational behaviour by owners and developers of land might hold back supply in anticipation of higher future prices, was ruled out, helping to explain Barker's lukewarm attitude to LVT. To obtain the recommendation in favour of new development taxes, Barker must be assuming that land-release incentives of a development tax for local authorities outweigh the disincentives to owners and that most of the revenue will be spent on new social housing.

The focus on new taxes on development would be reasonable if it simply involved a rationalisation of Section 106 of the 1990 Planning Act. However, the aim appears to be to extract additional planning gain from developers for local authorities and for central government. This could constitute an impediment to development, with long delays, rendering marginal schemes unviable. The Barker Review Final Report (2004) contains very optimistic assumptions about the likely success of new higher taxes. The past failure of such taxes was characterised by owners withholding land for development, expecting a future tax regime would be more favourable. This outcome seems a problem for the future too.

It is not clear against which benchmark is the gain to be measured. For example, suppose farmland with the expectation of planning approval, is sold to a developer or an intermediary. The uplift in value when permission is granted may only be a small fraction of the total uplift relative to the farmland price that would apply with no expectation of planning approval. If only the last stage is subject to taxation through the planning gain supplement, one might expect a new PGS minimising industry – land hedge funds – to arise, ensuring transactions take place as close as possible to the point before the planning decision is made. However, if earlier stages were to be taxed, chains of previous transactions would have to be traced and taxed, possibly after some years had elapsed. It would be difficult to draw the line that limits how far back this process could be taken.[36]

---

36 Given these difficulties, it is surprising that Barker recommended against the much simpler development tax measure of equalising VAT on new build (currently VAT exempt) and refurbishment.

Moreover, if the reforms were poorly phased, it is possible, in the short run, that the upheaval in the planning system could slow the rate of approvals. Owners and developers might restrain development because of the new development taxes, while demand for land rose in response to new money for real estate investment from the REITs and pension reform (permitting tax advantaged self-invested private pensions (SIPPs) to invest in real estate). Thus, rather than stabilising the market, instability might be exacerbated.

Conclusions

Property and land values are even more important in the economy with the liberalisation of domestic credit markets and international capital markets. With capital requirements on banks increasingly pro-cyclical under the Basel II Accords, stabilisation has become a very pressing macro-economic issue. Property and land values play extremely important roles in resource allocation both between locations, affecting income distribution and welfare, and for broad objectives such as housing supply. They also have a major influence on the distribution of purchasing power between individuals and between generations.

This paper has analysed the roles of property and land values in the economy and considered property tax reform from the point of view of the objectives of macro-economic stability, resource allocation, economic inequality and the environment. Concrete proposals for reform of Council Tax and the Uniform Business Rate have been put forward – with many more gainers than losers.

The Balance of Funding Review report of July 2004 recommended that council tax "be retained but reformed…to address its impact on those on low incomes and the impact of revaluation. Further work will be needed on the options for such reform." The reform criteria considered by the Review ignored issues of resource allocation for the regional or national economies, and macro economic stability issues, but noted that such considerations might be relevant in developing further proposals for reform. An independent inquiry to advise on council tax reform by Sir Michael Lyons to report by the end of 2005 offers the opportunity for the wider criteria discussed in this paper to be considered.[37]

There is much to be said in favour of ultimately giving the rate setting power for a reformed national property tax to the Bank of England, especially if the U.K. were to adopt the Euro, and the Bank had to give up its interest rate instrument. As explained in this paper, the impact of such a tax is very close to that of monetary policy on the household sector.

---

37 This inquiry was announced on July 20th 2005, after the publication of the Balance of Funding Review.

The Barker Review proposals of new development taxes of unknown scale and the recent tightening of Stamp Duty on the commercial sector, have alarmed stake-holders in the property sector. Thus, the moderate proposals made here for reforming UBR and at the same time reducing Stamp Duty and rationalising the existing development tax (Section 106) rather than bringing in new development taxes seem likely to meet little resistance. Property tax and planning reform together have the potential of releasing enormous long-term economic benefits for the U.K.

References

Abraham, J and Hendershott, P (1996). "Bubbles in Metropolitan Housing Markets". *Journal of Housing Research*, 7, 191-207.

Allsopp, C (2004). *Review of the Statistics for Economic Policymaking. Final Report.* London: HM Treasury.

Barker, K (2004). *Review of Housing Supply. Final Report.* London: HM Treasury.

Barker, K (2003). *Review of Housing Supply. Interim Report.* London: HM Treasury.

Bernanke, B and Blinder, A S (1992). "The Federal Funds Rate and the Channels of Monetary Transmission". *Journal of Economic Perspective*, 9(4), 27-48.

Bernanke, B and Gertler, M (1995). "Inside the Black Box: the credit channel of monetary policy transmission". *Journal of Economic Perspectives*, 9(4).

Bernanke, B; Gertler, M and Gilchrist, S (1996). "The financial accelerator and the flight to quality". *Review of Economics and Statistics*, 78(1), l-15.

Bernanke, B; Gertler, M and Gilchrist, S (1999). "The financial accelerator in a quantitative business cycle framework". *Handbook of Macroeconomics*, J. Taylor and Ml. Woodford (eds). New York: North-Holland.

Bowdler, C (2003). *Essays on inflation adjustment in open economies.* Oxford University DPhil thesis.

Cameron, G and Muellbauer, J (1998). "The Housing Market and Regional Commuting and Migration Choices." *Scottish Journal of Political Economy*, 54, 420-446.

Cameron, G and Muellbauer, J (1998). "Some Home Truths". *Financial Times*, August.

Cameron, G and Muellbauer, J (2000). "A Plague on most of our Houses." *Financial Times*, March.

Cameron, G and Muellbauer, J (2000). "Putting Property Tax on a Solid Footing." *The Guardian*, March.

Cameron, G and Muellbauer, J (2000). "Five Council Tax Reforms and Twelve Reasons to Enact Them." *New Economy*, June.

Cameron, G and Muellbauer, J (2001). "Earnings, Unemployment and Housing in Britain." *Journal of Applied Econometrics*, 16(3), 203-220.

Cheshire, P and Sheppard, S (2004). "The Introduction of Price Signals into Land Use Planning Decision-Making: a proposal." Mimeograph. London School of Economics, presented at ENHR Conference, Cambridge, July 3, 2004.

Danielsson, J (2003). "On the Feasibility of Risk Based Regulation." CESifo *Economic Studies*, 49, 157-179.

Engle, R F and Granger, C W J (1987). "Co-integration and error correction: Representation, estimation and testing." *Econometrica*, 55, 251-276.

Fernandez-Corugedo, E and Muellbauer, J (2004). "Consumer Credit Conditions in the U.K." *Bank of England Working Paper.*

Fisher, I (1933). "Debt Deflation Theory of Great Depressions." *Econometrica*, 1, 377-57.

Goodhart, C; Hofmann, B and Segoviano, M (2004). "Bank Regulation and Macroeconomic Fluctuations." *Oxford Review of Economic Policy*, 20(4).

Hendershott, P and McGregor, B D (2003). "Property Investor Rationality: evidence from U.K. capitalization rates." Mimeograph. Centre for Property Research, University of Aberdeen Business School.

HM Treasury (2003). *Housing, Consumption and EMU*. London: HM Treasury

HM Treasury (2003). *Submission on EMU from Leading Academics*. London: HM Treasury

HM Treasury (2003). *U.K. Membership of the Single Currency: an Assessment of the Five Economic Tests*. London: HM Treasury.

HM Treasury (2003). *Fiscal Stabilisation and EMU*. London: HM Treasury.

Hendry, D F (1995). *Dynamic Econometrics*. Oxford: Oxford University Press.

Hughes, G (1989). "The Switch from Domestic Rates to the Community Charge in Scotland." *Fiscal Studies*, 10(3), 1-12.

Hughes, G and McCormick, B (2000). *Housing Policy and Labour Market Performance.* London: Office of the Deputy Prime Minister.

Lyons, M (2004). *Independent Review of Public Sector Relocation*. London: HM Treasury.

Maclennan, D; Muellbauer, J and Stephens, M (1998). "Asymmetries in Housing and Financial Market Institutions and EMU." *Oxford Review of Economic Policy*: 14(3), 54-80.

Maclennan, D; Muellbauer, J and Stephens, M (2000). "Asymmetries in Housing and Financial Market Institutions and EMU." *Readings in Macroeconomics*, T Jenkinson (ed). Oxford: Oxford University Press.

McKinsey Global Institute (1998). *Driving Productivity Growth in the UK Economy.* Accessible online: www.mckinsey.com/mgi/publications/uk.asp.

McLean, I (2004). "Land tax: options for reform." Submission to ODPM Select Committee enquiry on The Balance of Funding Review. The University of Oxford.

Meen, G (1993). "The treatment of house prices in macro-econometric models: a comparison exercise." DOE Occasional Paper. Housing and Urban Monitoring and Analysis.

Meen, G (2003). "Regional Housing Supply Elasticities in England." Prepared for Barker Review of Housing Supply October 2003. The University of Reading.

Miles, D (2004). *The U.K. Mortgage Market: taking a longer-term view*. London: HM Treasury.

Muellbauer, J and Murphy, A (1997). "Booms and busts in the U.K. housing market." *The Economic Journal*, 107(November), 1701-27.

Muellbauer, J and Murphy, A (1994). "Explaining Regional House Prices in the U.K." Mimeograph. Nuffield College, The University of Oxford.

Muellbauer, J (2005). "Property Taxation and the Economy after the Barker Review." *Economic Journal*. 115(502), C99-C117.

Muellbauer, J (2002). "Safety in Property Tax." *Financial Times*, July.

Muellbauer, J (1997). "Rating the Housing Boom." *Observer*, May.

Muellbauer, J (1990). *The Great British Housing Disaster and Economic Policy*. London: Institute for Public Policy Research.

Muellbauer, J (1987). "The community charge, rates and tax reform." *Lloyds Bank Review*, October, 7-19.

(ODPM) Office of the Deputy Prime Minister (2003). *Sustainable Communities: Building for the Future*. London: Office of the Deputy Prime Minister.

(ODPM) Office of the Deputy Prime Minister (2004). *Balance of Funding Review – Report*. London: Office of the Deputy Prime Minister

Quang D A and Sirmans, C F (1994). "Residential Property Tax Capitalization: discount rate evidence from California." *National Tax Journal*, 47(2), 341-48.

Spencer, P (1988). "The Community Charge and Its Likely Effects on the U.K. Economy." Credit Suisse First Boston, June, 1-28.

Taylor, A and Goodhart, C (2004). "Procyclicality and Volatility in the Financial System: the Implementation of Basel II and IAS 39." Draft paper. *Financial Markets Group*, London School of Economics.

Weale, M (2003). "Commentary: the UK economy." *National Institute Economic Review*, 186(1), 4-7.

4 Commentary

Richard Brooks, Research Director, Fabian Societ

Are the taxes which are best economically, the worst politically? The philosophical and economic case for a land value tax (LVT) seems strong, but the issue has all the hallmarks of a political minefield: large numbers of people would be affected by any change; the status quo is seen to be unsatisfactory but there is little consensus about the appropriate response; and public understanding is low.

This response to the chapters by Iain McLean and John Muellbauer considers the political prospects for reform of land and property taxation, and is organised into three sections. The first section reviews pressing political issues to assess whether they can be used as opportunities to put LVT on the agenda. Second, who are the key constituencies or interest groups that would be affected by changes to the taxation of land and property? Finally, what could be done to make the introduction of LVT more politically attractive to a progressive government?

Pressing political issues

There are at least three current political issues to which LVT is relevant. First, the government has committed to re-valuing the Council Tax base in England. Second, a dangerous housing asset bubble has developed and affordability has become a problem for many people. Third, official reviews provide milestones for the LVT debate in the near future, including the report of the Lyons Inquiry into local government funding (Lyons Inquiry, 2004) and the government's response to the Barker Review of housing supply (Barker, 2004).

Re-valuation of the Council Tax base has been in the pipeline since the Local Government Act of 2000. Nonetheless, the full political implications have become widely recognised only in the last few years. Council Tax is currently charged, and local authority tax bases are calculated, on the basis of 1991 property valuations. Since that time there has been massive but uneven property price appreciation in the UK. If this appreciation had been uniform across the country then re-valuation might have relatively minor effects. However, since 1991 property values have increased far more in the Greater South East of England than in other areas such as the northern regions.

Using current property values, and re-setting the valuation bands so that the same number of properties are in each band before and after re-valuation, would cause a shift of the tax burden towards the areas which have had more appreciation. Crudely, the fiscal burden would shift south, at a time when there are 44 seats in the south east where Labour could lose to a swing of less than 2.5 per cent in the next general election (author's calculations from BBC figures). Large areas of the north of England would meanwhile have very high proportions of their homes in the lowest valuation bands. If re-valuation proceeds then the government will have to engage one way or the other with the difficulties of reforming land and property taxation.

One option for government in the face of the planned revaluation of Council Tax is to move land and property taxation away from its current form and towards a different system such as that represented by land value tax. However, the more progressive any new system is, the more disruption it is likely to cause – as more winners and losers will be created, and the losers are likely to protest more than the winner. Yet one of the advantages of LVT is precisely its progressivity relative to Council Tax. It is therefore probably not right to say that LVT offers government a way out of the re-valuation dilemma. Instead, the inevitable discussions around re-valuation present an opportunity to increase public and professional understanding of the potential merits of LVT. As Iain McLean's chapter points out, LVT has too often been seen as the preserve of 'enthusiasts' who can border on the obsessive. Council Tax revaluation offers, at the very least, the opportunity to broaden the community that has seriously engaged with the idea.

The second set of issues to which LVT is relevant is housing supply. Mortgage affordability remains relatively good for many existing borrowers due to low interest rates and healthy household incomes. However, property values are at historic highs as a multiple of household earnings, and first-time buyer numbers have fallen dramatically as home ownership moves out of their financial reach. The number of mortgage loans made each year to first time buyers remained remarkably stable from 1993 to 2002, averaging more than 500,000. In 2003 and 2004 the numbers of such loans was 360,000 in each year, a level not seen since 1991-1992, and before that 1980-1981 (Council of Mortgage Lenders, 2005). Professional opinions vary on the likely development of this scenario, with some predicting a 'soft landing' from current valuations, and others a harder fall. Avoiding the latter outcome will be one of the government's top priorities.

LVT appears to have real advantages in relation to increasing the responsiveness of housing supply to demand. As John Muellbauer indicates, LVT could reflect the opportunity costs of land use much better than the current arrangements. This would apply both to new developments, where it would act as an incentive to develop unused sites, and to existing properties, where it would incentivise 'under-occupiers' or 'under-utilisers' to release their property back into the market or make more efficient use of it. It is worth noting that the proposed Planning-gain Supplement would not incentivise either. This political problem with the latter effect, on domestic households in particular, is that it implies increased volatility of tenure: low income occupiers of high value land would effectively be forced to move. This is economically efficient but potentially politically difficult. The affected people would not just be 'Devon pensioners' but also probably highly indebted young families with large mortgages relative to their incomes, who are already near their financial limits. Moreover, there is a danger that it could conflict with the government's aim of promoting mixed communities, as high land value areas become only affordable to those on high incomes.

Finally, the Lyons Inquiry and Barker Review will both prompt public debates that will encompass the issue of land and property taxation. The Lyons Review was seen by many as a way of delaying difficult discussions about the future of local taxation until after the 2005 election, and is due to report by the end of 2005. The Labour Manifesto contained an explicit promise both to reform Council Tax (in the longer term) and to consider the conclusions of the Lyons Inquiry. The Barker Review of housing supply reported in 2004 with a series of recommendations to improve the responsiveness of housing supply, including ambitious house-building targets and proposals for the introduction of a Planning-gain Supplement, effectively a new tax on development. The government is due to reply to Barker Review by the end of 2005.

This alignment of issues – Council Tax revaluation, high house prices and Lyons/Barker – could either shut the door to future reform, or provide the impetus that has been missing from previous debates. It will be up to supporters of LVT to make the case for the latter.

Key stakeholders

Businesses, the property sector, public sector occupiers, and local authorities are all well organised to lobby and make their case to government. However, the most important stakeholders in the debate around LVT are taxpayers – the voting public. Most households currently pay Council Tax and most would be directly financially affected by its reform. Domestic property reform is thus the most politically sensitive aspect of the LVT debate.

No taxes are popular (with the exception, amongst most people, of taxes paid only by the very rich) but Council Tax appears to be particularly unpopular at the moment. This may be because it is felt to be unfair; or because it comes in a single annual bill in which increases are highly visible; or because few people understand what it pays for; or because it has gone up by significantly more than inflation in recent years; or even because it is so widely criticised by economists and other professional analysts.

However, none of this means that LVT would be more popular than Council Tax. In fact asset taxes more generally, including Stamp Duty, Inheritance Tax, and Capital Gains Tax appear to be particularly unpopular in the UK. The existing asset taxes are particularly visible because they are paid at very infrequent intervals – when somebody dies, when a housing transaction takes place, or when an asset is sold – and can be at high marginal rates. LVT would be paid regularly at a very low rate. Never the less, while LVT can claim convincing economic advantages over Council Tax and all of these, it cannot yet claim political advantages.

It is a key political consideration in any fiscal reform that winners stay quiet whilst losers complain, often noisily. This establishes a high hurdle for any fiscal reform that affects a large number of people. Even reforms which produce better outcomes overall and more winners than losers may be politically very difficult to implement. Any reform of Council Tax which addressed the highly regressive nature of the current system would generate large number of both winners and losers. Further, the winners and losers would be geographically concentrated, with most of the losers in the more affluent and often more politically marginal areas of England. Council Tax rates have also increased in recent years in a highly visible way, and the tax is becoming a serious target for the government's political opponents.

Turning to businesses, non-domestic rates (NDR) have not been a particularly contentious political issue since 1997. The system has not been structurally changed since its introduction in 1990, and unlike domestic properties, business properties have been regularly re-valued on a five year cycle. The problems that have been stored up in relation to Council Tax have thus been regularly defused in the non-domestic sector. In addition, annual increases in the charge per £ of rateable value for non-domestic property have been held to inflation, whilst the average increase in the rate of Council Tax has gone up faster than this. As a result the balance of local taxation has shifted from non-domestic property to households.

Developers (and land owners) currently contribute some of the land value increases associated with development through Section 106 agreements negotiated with local authorities, to mitigate the impact of new development on the local area. This will often take the form of developer contributions to new social housing or public infrastructure. The process is expensive and time consuming for all parties, highly variable across different authorities, and widely disliked on all sides. Developers could easily, therefore, be part of any constituency of change. At the same time there is growing recognition of the need for existing local communities to benefit from new development, partly as a way of securing their support for it. The Barker Review has proposed the introduction of a Planning-gain Supplement to simplify the process of quantifying the contributions made by developers. The exact level and form of such a supplement, its practicality, and crucially who would receive the funds, are all likely to be matters of significant controversy in the near future.

Finally local authorities and councillors have their own interests. At present Council Tax is the only fiscal instrument at the disposal of local authorities, although they are now allowed to trade and charge for various services. The form of local revenue-raising arrangements and their counterpart in the central government grant system are a subject of intense and continuing interest to the local government community. However, it has proved difficult for this group to transform public dissatisfaction with Council Tax into public support for any alternative system, and difficult also to provide any evidence that shifting the balance of funding from central grant towards locally raised revenue would be beneficial.

Implementing LVT will mean creating a sufficiently powerful constituency for change. A large part of the interests above will have to be converted, or, if that proves impossible, at the least neutralised as a source of opposition.

Preparing the ground

What could be done to ease the path for the introduction of LVT? A major change such as this will require a strong case that is robust to expert criticism, and convincing to the general public. At the moment public understanding is very low, and we are a long way from the political benefits appearing to outweigh the risks. Nonetheless, there are a number of ways this situation might change. Firstly, however, we must be sure to get the timing of any implementation right.

LVT offers a useful macro-economic stabilising mechanism, damping household spending capacity when it is buoyed up by property values and supporting it when values fall. It seems hard to deny that LVT could be better than current property taxation arrangements in this regard. However, the top of the housing cycle is probably the most politically difficult moment to introduce LVT, partly because its yield will be highest and partly because it might push some heavily mortgaged homeowners over the edge. There must be a concern that it would burst the balloon rather than ease the inevitable downwards adjustment. On the other hand, given the relatively long lead time before LVT could be introduced we are unlikely to be at the same point of the housing cycle at that time.

Moving on from these more esoteric debates, increasing public understanding is paramount. The discussion around LVT can become much more mainstream if its proponents are able to inject it into the forthcoming debates around the Lyons Inquiry, the government's response to the Barker Review, and the revaluation of the Council Tax base. There will have to be a long lead in to gain public consent and political will. The revaluation process should therefore probably be seen as a stage on the way to wider reform of local taxation as well as land and property taxation.

Some of the impacts of LVT could be softened, and even if this meant losing some of the economic benefits in the process the end result might still be better than the status quo. For example, low income households (or even all households) could be protected by a transition period during which they were sheltered from sharp increases in their tax liabilities. Elderly occupiers might be able to defer payment until after their death, although this might not impress them or their inheritors greatly.

Another option would be to introduce LVT such that it yielded less revenue than Council Tax in total, resulting in less domestic losers overall. This could be paid for by increasing the total revenue from non-domestic property. Alternatively the local tax base could be expanded to include a local income tax, although it would be politically extremely difficult to introduce this in a way that increased overall marginal tax rates.

Perhaps the most important thing would be a really clear understanding of what the household impacts might look like by income group, household type, and geographical area. This kind of work would allow the parameters of a politically plausible scheme to be determined. There is no clear formula for such a calculation, but very crudely, no scheme which appears to be financially detrimental to significant numbers of swing voters in marginal constituencies is politically plausible. This raises the possibility that Council Tax might endure in its present form. Although its failings are recognised there does not seem to be united political will for reform.

References

Barker, K (2004). *Barker Review of Housing Supply: securing our future housing needs. Final Report*. London: HM Treasury and Office of the Deputy Prime Minister.

Council of Mortgage Lenders (2005). *Loans for House Purchase: affordability and previous tenure.* Accessed online: www.cml.org.uk/servlet/dycon/zt-cml/cml/live/en/cml/xls_sml_ Table-PR2.xls

Lyons Inquiry (2004). *Lyons Inquiry into Local Government Funding*. Accessed online: www.lyonsinquiry.org.uk.

5 Summary of the seminar discussion

Karl Widerquist, Doctoral Candidate in Politics,
Lady Margaret Hall, Oxford University

The seminar 'Land Value Tax: worth the transition?' was attended by about 30 people, mostly academics, politicians, and policy advocates. The discussion, following presentations by McLean, Muellbauer, and Brooks, focused primarily on four issues: the advantages of Land Value Tax (LVT); the mix of central and local government control over such taxes; political concerns with LVT; and overcoming political resistance. This chapter is a summary of the discussion and does not necessarily represent the views of any of the pamphlet's authors.

The advantages of Land Value Tax

Many participants were keen to expand further on the benefits of LVT drawing on the three papers presented.

Economic efficiency.

A recent study in Oxfordshire argued that business and council tax could be replaced with an LVT of one percent. The report concluded this would deliver efficiency advantages and improve macroeconomic stability by reducing speculative fluctuations in asset prices.

Incentivising sustainable development.

LVT would give the owners of underused land an incentive to develop it, making more property available in city centres and reducing the need to build housing in satellite communities.

Funding public services.

One participant suggested that a tax on economic rent has virtually no deadweight loss, while the current tax system has a deadweight loss of nearly 30 pence in the pound. That means that public projects are inefficient unless their benefits are more than 30 per cent higher than their cost. If LVT can eliminate some of that that loss many more spending projects for better infrastructure, public transport, and public schools become tenable.

While this issue was not taken-up directly, there was some discussion of the politics of public service funding. Some argued that the argument for better-funded public projects will not appeal to all constituencies. People with neo-liberal values will resist anything that is justified on the grounds of larger public investment, as it implies smaller private investment. One response to this concern was that greater efficiency of tax collection means that we can get greater public investment out of the same amount of taxes and therefore with no additional loss in private investment.

Helping tenants

People who do not own property constitute one of the largest groups of potential winners from a switch to LVT. They make up 30 per cent of the country, and most of them have lower incomes than the other 70 per cent. The extent to which they stand to gain would depend on the ability of landlords to pass on the extra tax to tenants. However, if people are paying council taxes that will be replaced by a lower LVT rate, the shift will change the full after-tax rental value of land, and landlords may be able to increase rents by as much as people are saving in council taxes.

Not all renters are necessarily winners. Social tenants, who currently do not pay council tax, would probably see some amount of LVT passed on to them in the form of increased rent. It is not clear that social tenants should pay nothing towards LVT taxes, but we should be aware that they stand to lose out. Some argued that the housing benefit is the wrong solution for the housing problem, and that it has ballooned out of control. The problem is that some people cannot afford housing on the private market; the nation might be better off with an income support system to ensure that everyone can afford housing on the private market than with direct housing benefits.

Central or Local Government Control

The question of how much scope local governments would have to decide the level of land tax led into a more general discussion of how much power over tax rates the central government should grant to local authorities. Many expressed concerns that the current lack of connection between local planning decisions and local tax revenues causes problems. For instance, Britain currently has a uniform national business tax rate, with revenues taken by central government. The benefit of this system is that there is some redistribution from wealthier areas to relatively poor areas. But the centralisation of revenue reduces local authorities' incentives to increase their tax base. This is particularly true when political considerations are included: the opponents of planning decisions tend to be existing local residents, while many of the beneficiaries of new housing will not live locally. If there were more localisation of tax revenue, local authorities would have greater incentives to confront local opposition and widen their tax base without the increased revenue flowing to central government.

Set against this was a question over democratic legitimacy. Some argued that local governments have a short time horizon, lack accountability and would not consider long-term consequences of an excessively high a rate.

Others argued that there are genuine differences in opinion about the right level of tax: local authorities might want to experiment, and voters might then be able to hold them accountable for their decisions.

It was also observed that local authorities already have some incentive to increase their tax bases. The costs of the current system are so high that with a more efficient tax system it is possible to shift the balance toward local authorities without reducing equalisation.

One participant argued that equalisation has become a giant mammoth. Although poor local authorities need help, when it gets to the point that almost all local authorities get an equalisation grant from the central government it seems less a system of equalisation than a centralised system of funding.

Central government could stipulate and pay for local services up to a minimum standard and allow local governments to decide whether to have additional taxes and a higher level of service. However, such a system would have its own problems. 'Postcode lotteries' would put pressure on central governments to intervene and promote more uniform standards. This would at least lead to greater complexity and may actually require a further shift towards centralisation. Others argued that if local areas did have more responsibility they would be held accountable for differences in standards through the ballot box.

One participant asked why we should make major changes in the balance of funding when there is no evidence that more local funding will improve outcomes. Local government advocates have been unable to prove that better government results from increased local funding. For instance, some areas raise 10 per cent of their own revenue; some raise 50 per cent of their revenue; but there are no great differences in voter turnout between areas with greater and lesser control of their own revenue.

Others countered that one should not expect that the balance of funding and voter turnout would be related, when all the local government authorities have very limited power over what they do with their revenue even if they raise it themselves. There is evidence that voters are affected by local government power. For example, destruction of local government in Norway greatly increased dissatisfaction with government.

Concerns with authors' proposals

Distortions

Several participants were concerned that both McLean and Muellbauer proposed very different tax rates for residential and business property. Distortions result whenever two different uses of the same asset are taxed differently. Enormous incentive problems can arise as people want to convert property from business use to residential use to avoid the tax. People will have incentives to specify the minimum number of days per year a must person sleep (or maximum amount of business she can conduct) in a building for it to be considered a residence. The different tax rates also raises issues of fairness. For example, the owner of a small grocery store in an area of expensive residential housing will be paying a higher tax rate on his land than his wealthy clients pay on theirs.

Political feasibility

Some participants worried that LVT is an example of 'Stern's Law', which states that the best taxes economically are the worst politically, but the Danish land tax was held up as a positive example of a way around Stern's law. The Danes overcome the financial leverage problem with yearly revaluations. However, even this Danish approach has run into some problems as adjustments in taxes have been suspended due to high land price rises. It was suggested that was partly a way to reduce the effective property tax, in response to the downturn in the Eurozone in recent years.

Resistance

One source of political resistance to LVT is the fact that there are pensioners with very low incomes but very valuable property who would be hard hit by the land tax. The Danes allow pensioners to defer property taxes until their property is sold, usually at death. This makes the tax of low importance to pensioners, but not to their heirs who had developed the expectation of receiving a large inheritance. Given that most inheritors will be in their 40s and 50s, and will themselves have benefited greatly from the upturn in property values, some felt that it was harder to feel as sorry for them as for the young who are priced out of owning homes.

One major area of concern was that any fundamental change in the tax system creates winners and losers, and losers will put up political resistance. Even if LVT has enormous advantages once it is established, the beneficiaries of future stability and efficiency do not constitute an interest group. The people who will lose out in a tax shift do constitute a group; they know who they are and what they will lose, and they are capable organizing a political opposition to the change.

Overcoming political resistance

The seminar ended on a positive note with a discussion of how to overcome political resistance. Political resistance – even to beneficial changes – is a reason why the politics of LVT must not begin with a discussion of the efficacy of land taxes themselves, but with the existing system of raising revenue. If the current system is fine, why change? The present way of raising revenue creates heavy deadweight loses – environmentally, socially, and economically – and if this fact is recognised the introduction of LVT might become what the Americans call a 'no brainer'. Council tax hastily came into being because the poll tax was so unpopular. If weaknesses of council tax system are exposed, and if it becomes increasingly unpopular, the possibility of shifting to LVT becomes much more real.

Another proposed response to the problem of political resistance by losers was that the government could link LVT with an easing of planning restrictions. This would give property owners more freedom to invest in improving their property. So, although taxes on land value will be higher, the investment value of land will also be higher compensating property owners for the increased taxes they will pay at no cost to government revenue.

LVT could also be introduced slowly, giving people time to adjust their behaviour. From the time of introduction onwards, yearly revaluations would help because they would be more incremental than revaluations every five years. The problem with losers resisting changes will be smaller if the changes are small and predictable. Therefore, many participants agreed that we do not need to seek one large change that will make for a perfect system; even a halfway measure would be a big improvement.

6 Conclusion

Dominic Maxwell and Anthony Vigor, Institute for Public Policy Research

Many will bemoan the apparently political decision in September to postpone the revaluation of Council Tax until after the next general election. Here we argue that this decision presents an opportunity, not just to rethink the role of local government but the nature of the property taxation system. Much of the policy debate will focus on the appropriate balance between local and central tax raising powers. We argue that the time is now right for radical reform of property taxation and Land Value Taxation should be considered as part of a reformed system.

Politicians are understandably very wary about significant changes to the taxation system and the difficulties surrounding the Poll Tax and Council Tax revaluation aptly demonstrate how fraught this area is. It is also increasingly clear that the current system of property taxation in the UK is unfair, militates against macroeconomic stability and does not adequately promote the government's housing and development policy objectives.

The previous chapters have demonstrated the potential benefits of Land Value Taxation within a reformed system. Iain McLean and John Muellbauer both have proposals for intermediate steps. McLean suggests that the current property tax for businesses, National Non-Domestic Rates, should be entirely converted to a local land tax. For domestic property taxation, he acknowledges that, although the case for Land Value Taxation is strong, the political problems of transition are difficult.

Muellbauer would shift only half the basis of National Non-Domestic Rates to land tax, keeping the other half on property. Rather than a local tax, Muellbauer's Land Value Taxation would be national. He suggests combining it with a property tax of around half of one per cent, to replace Council Tax.

The gap between theory and policy is particularly wide in the case of Land Value Taxation. Previous chapters, especially Richard Brooks', highlight some of the potential pitfalls. Three issues are particular pertinent: the knock-on consequences for the rest of the tax system, which always include an element of unpredictability; the difficult question of asset-rich income-poor pensioners, who are unlikely to be satisfied simply by the option to postpone payment; and the concentration of people who would be worse off who live in marginal seats.

These are issues that should be actively considered within the Lyons Inquiry's newly expanded remit. The inquiry will finally report towards the end of 2006 to inform the Comprehensive Spending Review of 2007.

This is not to argue that the Lyons Inquiry should recommend the wholesale replacement of property taxation with a Land Value Tax, as the 'whole hoggers' (Andelson, 2000) are pressing for. Rather, it could do the work necessary to get government into a position where Land Value Taxation becomes a detailed and reasonable option for long-term reform. As the previous chapters have demonstrated, Land Value Taxation provides the opportunity to address many of the issues that Lyons will be considering: it could be firmly tied to local decision-making; it would be a buoyant tax, so would rise automatically (and, crucially, predictably) when land values rise; and it would sharpen the incentives to use land efficiently, both for new buildings and for the existing stock (which comprises 99 per cent of effective supply).

More immediate reforms are also possible, and could secure some of the main advantages of LVT while avoiding the worst transitional and political costs. This means aiming to:

- Align the incentives of planners and local residents, so that the benefits of development are felt by local communities.
- Secure funding for infrastructure by capturing uplifts in land value.
- Better reflect land prices across time and between areas, to contribute to macroeconomic stability and resource allocation.

More specifically, we recommend the following.

- The government should use the opportunity of the Lyons Inquiry to set a clear direction for longer-term reform of property taxation, alongside local government function and funding. This should include a serious and detailed consideration of Land Value Taxation.
- The proposed Planning-gain Supplement should be used as a way of establishing the principle that some increases in value arise from public action, rather than private, and that it is therefore legitimate for it to be used for the public good.
- If council tax is retained, even as an interim measure, future revaluation should occur every one or two years, with more bands. This would help create an automatic stabiliser for the housing market, and ensure property taxes respond better to differences over time, between regions and between properties.
- Letting pensioners defer property tax until they move house or die is a promising option, although more analysis is needed of who would benefit, and how much it would have to be funded by government.
- Reassessing the role of equalisation grants would allow more space for local authorities to capture the gains from development in their area,

and give them the incentives to make sure such developments are possible.

- In the longer term, a change in the tax system presents an opportunity to iron out the arbitrary jumps in stamp duty.

There is a growing consensus that property taxation needs reform. This pamphlet has argued that adopting elements of Land Value Taxation could help in the reforms of Council Tax, local government finance, planning and housebuilding, as well as promoting macroeconomic stability. Introducing any changes will require long-term planning, detailed economic and distributional analysis – and, above all, political courage. But, with vision and patience, a consensus is possible. Now is the time to seek it.

References

Andelson, R V (2000). "Introduction", in Andelson RV (ed) *Land-Value Taxation Around the World.* Third Edition. Oxford: Blackwell.